William Andrews, George Smith Tyack

Bygone Church Life in Scotland

William Andrews, George Smith Tyack

Bygone Church Life in Scotland

ISBN/EAN: 9783743346086

Manufactured in Europe, USA, Canada, Australia, Japa

Cover: Foto ©ninafisch / pixelio.de

Manufactured and distributed by brebook publishing software (www.brebook.com)

William Andrews, George Smith Tyack

Bygone Church Life in Scotland

BYGONE CHURCH LIFE IN SCOTLAND.

Glasgow Cathedral
with Blacader's Aisle

D Small

Bygone Church

Life in Scotland

Edited by

William Andrews . . .

LONDON :

WILLIAM ANDREWS & CO., 5, FARRINGDON AVENUE, E.C.

1899.

WILLIAM·ANDREWS·&·C^O

⚘ THE·HULL·PRESS ⚘

GIFT

Preface.

I HOPE the present collection of new studies on old themes will win a welcome from Scotsmen at home and abroad.

My contributors, who have kindly furnished me with articles, are recognized authorities on the subjects they have written about, and I think their efforts cannot fail to find favour with the reader.

WILLIAM ANDREWS.

THE HULL PRESS,
Christmas Eve, 1898.

595

Contents.

to render "the King's Daughter" yet more
"glorious within" by stripping her of every
shred of her "clothing of wrought gold."
Religion, that it might be more truly spiritual,
was to be sent forth into the world absolutely
naked of every external sign or form. The
furniture of the churches was torn out, and sold
or burnt; the statues of the saints were of
course broken up; but the organs were also
pulled down, and even the carved stalls and
screens of the cathedrals were declared to be
"idolatrous." Nothing illustrates more strongly,
and more curiously, the indiscriminate frenzy of
destruction which for a time took possession of
the people, than the fact that monuments and
tombstones were even condemned as superstitious and sinful. Only a comparatively few
of all the many memorials of Scottish worthies
of earlier centuries escaped demolition, and this
not wrought by the mere violence of a turbulent
mob, but by formal resolutions of the General
Assembly in the seventeenth century. In 1640
the Kirk Session of Aberdeen ordered the
removal of a portrait of "Reid of Pitfoddels"
from the vestry of the church, on the ground
of its "smelling somewhat of Popery"; and in

1649 a similar authority at Kilmarnock condemned "a graven image" on the tomb of Lord
Boyd. This action was taken, no doubt, in
obedience to the summons issued by the
General Assembly in 1640 to the presbyteries
to complete the removal and destruction of all
monuments.

Such being the state of feeling in Scotland,
we are not surprised to find that the sign of
our salvation was found even more obnoxious
by the leaders of the movement there than it
was among their brethren in England. With
the latter, when the interiors of the churches
were swept bare of crosses, the passion for
destruction was stayed so far as that emblem
was concerned; on spire and gable, on tomb
and tablet, in churchyard and market-place,
the stone crosses were for the most part left;
and even when, under the Puritan regime of
the following century, an attempt was made to
pull down these by Parliamentary authority,
the popular feeling was so far from being
strongly in its favour, that the work was by
no means done thoroughly and completely.

In spite of all that was intended, and even
attempted, Scotland has, nevertheless, retained

some examples of the ancient crosses, which are well worthy of our attention. In remote places the sacred sign has been spared in scattered instances for more appreciative days; in more populous centres the cross has been preserved in a secularised form, its symbol gone, and with it its meaning; but amid the wreck of so much, we must receive gratefully the fragments that remain.

The strictly church crosses, those that once stood on altar or on rood-screen, that led the stately procession, or cast their benign shadows athwart the graves of the faithful—these were all swept away. The Synod of Fife held, at the time of the Reformation, "visitations" from time to time, to search out and remove "crosier staffes" and "divers crosses," as well as other ancient furniture, from the parish churches; and in so doing, doubtless, it was but acting as the other Synods of the country did. The old crosses in the churchyards, many of them of great age, and probably most interesting pieces of sculpture, were almost all destroyed. The market crosses, however, have in several cases survived, although the national emblem, the unicorn, has usurped the place of the

Christian symbol, the cross; and the attack upon mortuary memorials was not altogether successful; in fact, it was hardly to be expected that any people would consent to the entire obliteration of the grave-stones of their ancestors.

The most famous existing example is the High Cross, or Market Cross, of the capital. The date of the foundation of this structure is unknown. Not far from its site is an ancient well, known as the Cross Well, from which some have conjectured that possibly the earliest cross was reared by some unknown teacher of the faith, who, in a far distant age, established himself in a cell beside this clear spring. Such a spot, we know, was often chosen by these apostolic teachers, and not infrequently a rude cross, erected hard by, served to mark the place as, in some sort, a sanctuary. Our first authentic allusion to this Cross is, however, of a date some centuries later than this. In 1175 William the Lion (1165-1214) decreed that "all merchandisis salbe presentit at the mercat and mercat croce of burghis." From this, we may safely conclude that Edinburgh had a recognised Market Cross by that date, since we can hardly imagine that the capital was without a symbol that was evidently usual in the burghs of the country. A reference to the Cross is supposed to be contained in a document of 1437. The assassins of the noble but unfortunate King James I., who was barbarously slain in the February of that year, are said to have suffered for their crime "mounted on a pillar in the market-place in Edinburgh." Ten years later we meet with a definite reference to this structure; the Charter of St Giles's Church, dated 1447, contains the words "ex parte occidentali fori et crucis dicti burgi," on the west side of the market-place and of the Cross of the said burgh. King James III. (1460-1488), in an epistle to the citizens of his capital written in October 1477, ordains that "all pietricks, pluvaris, capones, conyngs, checkins, and all other wyld foulis and tame to be usit and sald about the Market Croce and in na other place." At this time, therefore, we find the Cross established as an acknowledged centre for commercial Edinburgh, such as it was in the fifteenth century.

The exact form of this early Market Cross is as doubtful as the date of its foundation. The pillar of the present erection is the same as that in the earliest historical notices which we have of it; but whether this originally stood upon a

simple pedestal, upon a pyramid of steps, or
upon an elevated platform like that of a later
date, we cannot say. It has been thought
probable, however, that the Cross was raised to
its dignified altitude by the addition of the
arcaded platform in the time of James III.
This monarch was indolent, and unfit for the
rule of a somewhat turbulent kingdom, but he
was a patron of the arts, and a friend of the
Church. Several improvements were made in
Edinburgh during his reign, including the en-
largement of St Giles's Cathedral; hence it is
possible that he also took in hand the adornment of the neighbouring Cross. Under James
VI., previously to his becoming Sovereign of
Great Britain, further alterations were made.
In 1555 we read of work at the Cross consisting
of "bigging the rowme thereof," which is supposed to mean that at this time the open arches
which upheld the platform were filled in, so as
to form an enclosed "rowme" below. This
room was entered by a door, which was secured
with a lock; so that thenceforward only those
having some high and official duty to perform,
such as publishing a royal proclamation, could
ascend to the broad base of the Cross. In the

City Treasurer's accounts for 1560 are two entries as follows: "Item for ane band to ye Croce dur," and "Item for mending of ye lok of ye Croce dur." Once more, we read in the same records for 1584, "5 Julii, Item, ye sam day given for ane lok to ye Croce dur, and three keyis for it." There is extant an old engraving giving a bird's-eye view of Edinburgh in 1647, from which we may see that in its main outlines the Market Cross was then much as it is to-day; the summit of the shaft (from which, doubtless, the cross had already been flung down) having been surmounted by the heraldic symbol of Scotland at the date of the last-quoted entry from the city accounts. The record concerning it is of a sum "payit to David Williamson for making and upputting of the Unicorn upon the head of the Croce."

Early in the next century the whole erection was moved to a new site. In 1617 it was "translated by the devise of certain mariners of Leith from the place where it stood past the memory of man to a place beneath in the High Street." A new substructure was made for it, of stone "brocht from the Deyne"; and the shaft was swung into "the new seat" on the

25th March, the cost of the entire work being £4486, 5s. 6d. (Scots).

The republicans of the Commonwealth period defaced the Cross, tearing down the royal arms, and hanging the crown from the head of the unicorn upon the gallows. At the Restoration, therefore, certain repairs had to be made; Robert Mylne was entrusted with the work, and a further contract was made with George Porteous " for painting the Croce."

During the succeeding century frequent complaints were made that the Cross was an obstruction to traffic; and at last in 1756 the complainants obtained their wish. On the 13th March in that year the Market Cross of Edinburgh was demolished. The pillar, which fell and broke during the operation, was sold to Lord Somerville, who set it up in the vicinity of his house at Drum; the medallions which had adorned the base came eventually into the hands of Sir Walter Scott, who built them into a wall at Abbotsford, where they remain; the site was marked out with stones, as some small compensation for the loss to the lovers of antiquity; and finally a plain stone pillar was erected beside the well hard by, and this was

officially declared to be from that day forward
the Market Cross of the city. Even this con-
temptible substitute was not, however, suffered
long to remain; but on the same plea of obstruction was presently removed like the Cross
itself.

The citizens of the ancient city did not unani-
mously concur, by any means, in this destruction
of a time-honoured landmark in the history of
the country; and efforts were repeatedly made
to obtain its restoration. After a time the movement was so far successful as to gain the return
of "the pillar of the Cross" to Edinburgh,
where it was set up on a pedestal within the
railings of St Giles's Church. So matters stood
until recent times, when a complete restoration
was effected by the generosity of the late Rt.
Hon. W. E. Gladstone, who built a new and
imposing octagonal base, on one of the faces
of which the following inscription was placed
in Latin, "Thanks be to God, this ancient
monument, the Cross of Edinburgh, devoted of
old to public functions—having been destroyed
by evil hands in the Year of our Salvation
1756, and having been avenged and lamented,
in song both noble and manly, by that man of

highest renown, Walter Scott—has now, by permission of the city magistrates, been rebuilt by William E. Gladstone, who, through both parents claims a descent entirely Scottish. November 23rd, in the Year of Grace 1885." The date is that of the day on which this noble present was formally given to the civic authorities by Mr Gladstone, who was then member of Parliament for Midlothian.

So far of the history of the fabric of the Cross : to trace in detail the great events in which it has been called to play a part, would be to recount no small portion of the annals of the Scottish kingdom. This spot has long been treated as the very centre and heart of the country. Here Scottish sovereigns met the citizens of their capital ; here proclamation was made of peace and war, of the accession of kings, and of aught else of prime and pressing interest to the people ; here, too, many have suffered for their devotion to causes, political or religious, which had—at any rate for a time—fallen before superior force.

A fountain near the old Cross ran red with wine when James IV. of Scotland brought home his bride, Margaret of England, and the first link in the golden chain was forged which should

shortly join the realms. Here in 1512 the royal
summons was read for the mustering of that
army, so many of the gallant members of which
were to fall at Flodden ; and here—most fate-
ful of all proclamations published there — the

EXECUTION OF THE EARL OF ARGYLE,
SHEWING THE OLD HIGH CROSS, EDINBURGH.

death of Elizabeth was announced, and the
accession of James VI. to the double Crown of
Great Britain.

John Knox was burnt in effigy at the Cross in

1555, when he failed to return from Geneva in answer to a summons from the bishops; and ten years later a Roman Catholic Priest was "tyed to the Cross" and pelted because he had dared to say Mass on Easter Day. The Earl of Morton was beheaded here in 1581. Under James the Seventh of Scotland and Second of England many a powerful head fell on the scaffold beneath the shadow of the Cross. Those were stormy times in which religion and politics were curiously and unhappily mingled, so that those who to one side seemed mere rebels, to the other appeared as martyrs. Among others who suffered was the Earl of Argyle, together with many of his clan who had been led by him to open revolt.

Edinburgh had another Cross, known as St John's, situated in the Canongate; it was similar in design to the High Cross, but smaller.

The Crosses of the Metropolis seem to have been taken as models by other Scottish burghs. Their plan was quite unlike any existing examples in England. The base or pedestal was an elevated platform, supported either by open arches, or by solid walls; on the top of this, the tall shaft of the cross was placed, and

latterly it was crowned by a unicorn holding
the Scottish shield. Steps, within the base, led
to the platform from which proclamations and
official notices were published by the city
heralds. Judging from the analogy of the Market
Crosses in the southern kingdom, it seems
probable that the base was originally intended
to be open, so as to afford shade or shelter, as
the weather might require, to some at least of
the market folk. Many English Crosses, the
best known example of all, for instance, that of
Chichester, provide accommodation of this sort,
but none of them have a flat roof serving as a
platform. Subsequently, as the business of the
country grew, this shelter would prove so in-
adequate as not to be worth considering ; and
then the lower structure was in some cases built
in, so as to protect the access to the platform,
reserved now for formal and official purposes
only.

   The city of Aberdeen boasts that her Market
Cross is the finest in the land. It was built in
1688 by a country mason named John Mont-
gomery, and was placed opposite the Tolbooth.
In 1842 it was moved to the present site in
Castle Street, and was at the same time some-

what altered. It is hexagonal in plan, six wide arches supporting the upper platform, round which runs a circular balustrade garnished with shields of arms and medallions of Scottish kings. The pillar rising from the midst is handsomely carved, and supports a unicorn in white marble holding the national shield. All the British sovereigns since its erection have been proclaimed from this Cross, as well as the two Pretenders in 1715 and 1745. Near the spot now occupied by this erection originally stood the Flesh Cross, close to which were the shambles; lower down Castle Street was the Fish Cross, or Laich Cross, indicating the position of the fish market.

Prestonpans possesses a Market Cross of the same type as those already described, and still in good condition, as also does Elgin; similar Crosses at Perth and Dundee have been unhappily destroyed. Amongst other notices of the Town Cross at Linlithgow is a record of punishment inflicted upon an unfortunate burgess, for "in his great raschness and suddantie destroying the head of the Toun's drum." This unmusical citizen was deprived of the freedom of the burgh, fined £50 Scots, and ordered to

"sitt doune upon his knees at the Croce at ten
houres before noone, and crave the provost,
baillies, and counsall pardone." Drums were
evidently of more account in Scotland in the
seventeenth century than crosses or tombstones.

The ceremony of beating the bounds, or as it
is called in Scotland "riding the marches," is
still observed in some burghs, and the procession
usually starts and terminates at the Cross if there
be one. At Lanark before separating the company sings "Scots wha hae" beneath the Cross,
near which stands what would two centuries
since have been called "an idolatrous statue" of
William Wallace. At Linlithgow the function
begins by drinking the sovereign's health at the
Cross, and the procession returns thither before
breaking up. At Kilmarnock Fastern's Eve (in
English, Shrove Tuesday) used to be celebrated
by a large amount of horse-play round the
ancient Cross ; the town fire-engines and their
hose being called into requisition for the drench-
ing of the crowd with water, who probably
drenched themselves with something rather
stronger later in the day.

Of all the royal edicts proclaimed from these
Crosses the following was certainly one of the

most curious. It was ordered to be published from every Town Cross in Scotland in 1619, and was issued by King James from London, whither a host of adventurers from his northern dominions had promptly followed him. The proclamation warns "all manner of persons from resorting out of Scotland to this our kingdome, unlesse it be gentlemen of good qualitie, merchands for traffiques, or such as shall have a generall license from our Counselle of that Kingdome, with prohibitioun to all masters of shippes that they transport no such persons;" it further goes on to announce that "Sir William Alexander, Master of Requests, hath received a commission to apprehend and send home, or to punish all vagrant persons who came to England to cause trouble, or bring discredit on their country."

Here and there throughout Scotland crosses of various kinds have no doubt escaped destruction, when they happen to be in obscure places, or small and scarcely noticeable in form or situation ; thus the old Cathedral of Brechin still preserves one of the consecration Crosses, cut in its walls as part of the ceremony of its original dedication. But almost the only examples of

importance left to us, besides those town crosses
which we have considered, are several exceedingly interesting ancient memorial or sepulchral
crosses, of which those at Iona are by far the
best known.

An anonymous writer in 1688, speaking of
this sacred isle, says, " that M'Lean's Cross is
one of the 360 standing before the Reformation ;
the others were thrown into the sea by order
of the Synod of Argyle." In the absence of
anything beyond the bare assertion, this statement
must be considered as at least doubtful. No
earlier writers, including those who had visited
Iona, mention the fact ; and if an organized
attack of this kind were made upon the monuments
of the island, it is difficult to explain why two
were left untouched. That there were many
more Crosses here formerly may be taken for
certain, and that the Synod of Argyle would
think them all idolatrous is equally clear ; but
it is not likely that it ordered so great an undertaking as that of digging from their foundations
nearly four hundred massive blocks of stone,
some, to judge by what is left to us, of great
size, and casting them into the sea. All such
monuments having been formally condemned

throughout Scotland, it is fair to assume that those of Iona met with a good deal of ill-usage. The "axes and hammers" of the isle would be brought to bear upon " the carved work thereof " ; and it is more probable that the mode of destruction has been of this kind, aided by time and

ST. MARTIN'S CROSS, IONA.

storm, whose ravages nothing has been attempted to stay or to repair, than that any definite scheme of demolition has been carried out.

Two fine crosses yet remain in good preservation in Iona, known respectively as St. Martin's

Cross and the Cross of the Maclean. The former of these is considerably the older, and stands in front of the ruined cathedral. It is a monolith measuring fourteen feet in height above ground, eighteen inches in breadth, and ten inches in thickness, and is set in a block of granite three feet in height. It is elaborately carved, figures of the Blessed Virgin - Mother and the Holy Child, of ecclesiastics in vestments, of musicians with harps and wind instruments, occupying one face, together with foliage and twining snakes; while the other has a more conventional design. On the roadside, near the ancient nunnery, stands Maclean's Cross, which has been described as "one of the oldest Celtic crosses in Scotland," and even as "the oldest Christian monument" in that country. This is to ascribe to an un-doubtedly ancient relic an antiquity to which it has no claim; it dates probably from the fifteenth century. It is eleven feet high, and is carved with the figure of the crucified Redeemer, attended by angels, and with much graceful scroll-work. The claimants for the greater age of this fine cross assert that it marks the spot where St. Columba rested on his last walk about the monastic lands.

St. Oran's Chapel, alleged to have been built by Queen Margaret some time after 1072, contains one or two broken crosses. There is the shaft of one erected in memory of the Abbot Mackinnon in 1489, a portion of another known now as the "Flat stone of Oran," and a fragment of yet a third. The famous burial ground of Iona, the Reilig Orain, to which were brought the remains of kings, not only from the mainland of Scotland, but from Ireland and even from Norway, has several sepulchral slabs which still bear the sacred sign. One, probably of the twelfth century, has a well-designed interlaced cross stretching almost the whole length and breadth of the stone, with a galley carved upon the one side of it and a sword upon the other; another, alleged to commemorate Ranald, Lord of the Isles in the early thirteenth century, has a small interlaced cross upon one side of a sword, and two "disguised" crosses, somewhat of the fylfot shape, upon the other. There is also a broken stone, with a portion of a cross of Irish design, and a fragmentary inscription. It has been supposed to mark the burial-place of Maol Patrick O'Banan, the saintly bishop of Conor and Down, who died in Iona in

1174.* Two boulders, measuring rather less
than two feet in length, have also been found in
the island, each incised with a cross. One, which
has a well - proportioned figure of the type
commonly called "runic," is supposed by some
to have been the stone, which, according to
his biographer Adamnan, formed the pillow of
St. Columba.

Some others of the Western Isles have preserved a few of their ancient crosses. Boswell,
in his "Journal of a Tour to the Hebrides" in
1773, speaks thus of the approach to Rasay:
"Just as we landed I observed a cross, or rather
the ruins of one, upon a rock, which had to me
a pleasing vestige of religion." A few days
later the traveller set out to explore the island,
and he made other discoveries of the same
nature. "On one of the rocks just where we
landed," he tells us, "there is rudely carved a
square, with a crucifix in the middle : here, it
is said, the Lairds of Rasay, in old times, used
to offer up their devotions ; I could not approach
the spot without a grateful recollection of the
event commemorated by this symbol." A little

* "Iona : its History, Antiquities, etc.," by Rev. A. MacMillan
and Robert Brydall, 1898.

further on he writes, " The eight crosses, which
Martin mentions as pyramids for deceased ladies,
stood in a semicircular line, which contained
within it the chapel ; they marked out the
boundaries of the sacred territory, within which
an asylum was to be had ; one of them, which
we observed upon our landing, made the first
point of the semicircle ; there are few of them
now remaining." On the islet of Oronsay,
immediately to the south of Colonsay, is a Celtic
cross with a Latin inscription, erected in memory
of a Prior who died in 1510. Some of the
crosses from Iona are said to have been carried
to the neighbouring island of Mull, and to the
mainland of Argyle. At Campbelltown in that
county is a handsome cross, carved from a
monolith of blue granite, and now serving as a
Market Cross, which is alleged to be one of the
spoils of St. Columba's isle.

Argyleshire has also preserved some interesting sculptured tombstones. The churchyard of
Kilfinan has two such ; one is adorned with a
wheel - headed cross, the shaft of which is
covered with scrolls, a wicker-pattern design
running down either side of it ; the other has
a cross with deep hollows at the intersection

of the arms. At Nereabolls, in Islay, is the
upper portion of a crucifix, broken off beneath
the arms of the figure; it is roughly carved,
but has nothing of the grotesqueness of some
very early attempts at the human form. All
these stones date from the fourteenth or following
century.

In certain districts several Celtic crosses have
been suffered to survive, or have been brought
forth from the concealment into which the
neglect, or the violence, of past ages had
thrown them; and they present perhaps the
most valuable examples of runic inscriptions
and of contemporary carving which we now
have in Great Britain. Some of them are
quadrilateral slabs on which the sacred symbol
is cut, others are carved into the shape of a
cross; most of them have a large amount of
characteristic adornment. There are men riding
and hunting, animals conventional, if not actually
grotesque, interlaced chain designs, and intricate
and often very graceful scrolls. Among other
figures cut on these ancient monuments we
find constantly repeated some of those Pictish
symbols, the meaning of which is one of the
apparently insoluble problems of archæology.

The twin circles connected by three lines like a Z, or included within the arms of it, the crescent crossed by two lines forming a V, a grotesque somewhat distantly resembling an elephant; these and other forms constantly meet us. They are characteristic of the carving of a time not more than eight or nine centuries from our own, yet the very alphabet of the symbolic language which they speak is lost. They have been described as the work of Cymric Christians, as Gnostic, as magical, as derived from oriental Paganism, as learned from Scandinavian heathenism; but even if we could agree as to their origin, we should yet be in the dark as to their meaning. In Wigtonshire are several crosses, including some of this type : we find them at Kirkcolm, Kirkmadrine, Whithorn, Monreith, and St. Ninian's cave. At Kirkcolm is an exceedingly rudely carved crucifix; beneath the figure of the Crucified is another human figure accompanied by two creatures meant apparently for birds; the whole being of the roughest description. The Monreith Cross stands seven and a quarter feet in height, and has a wheel head, with a shaft whose sides curve slightly outwards from top and bottom; an ingeniously contrived scroll covers the face. The Kirk-madrine example has incised upon it the sacred monogram XP conjoined, and arranged cross-wise within a circle.

In Kirkcudbright is the splendid Ruthwell Cross, standing over seventeen feet in height. The shaft tapers gracefully towards the head, and has within panels upon it the effigies of several saints; the sides have a singularly fine scroll of conventional foliage with birds; and the head is light and elegant. It is altogether a very beautiful structure.

Other stones worthy of notice now are, or have been found, at St Madoes and Dupplin, near Perth; at Kirriemuir, and elsewhere, in Forfar; and in some other places, chiefly along the north-eastern coast of the country. It must be remembered that the Reformation progressed much more slowly in the Highlands than in the Lowlands, so that we might naturally expect that the demolition of the crosses would not be carried out quite so thoroughly in the north as in the south.

It was, however, in a southern town that we read of the last use, until recent times, of that ancient ceremony for Good Friday which our forefathers called "Creeping to the Cross." On May 8th, 1568, Grindal, then bishop of London, writes to Sir William Cecil, afterwards Lord Burleigh : "Evans, who is thought a man of more simplicity than the rest, hath reported (as I am credibly informed) that at Dunbar, on Good Friday, they saw certain persons go bare-foot and bare-legged to the church, to creep to the cross ; if it be so the Church of Scotland will not be pure enough for our men."

In spite of the abolition of the sign of the cross in the ceremonial of the church, and the destruction, so far as possible, of the material cross in its buildings, even Presbyterian Scotland could not discard the emblem of St. Andrew from among its national devices. The Covenanters marched across the Border in the Great Civil War, under a flag which bore that symbol; the white Cross of St. Andrew lay athwart its field, charged at the centre with the thistle, while in the spaces between the four members of the cross was the motto, "Covenants for Religion, Croune, and Kingdoms.". Under the Commonwealth the royal arms, of course,

dropt out of use, their place being taken by a
shield, the first and fourth quarters of which
were charged with St. George's Cross (for
England), the second with St. Andrew's Cross
(for Scotland), and the third with the Irish
harp.

Some few folk-customs, involving the use

COVENANTER'S FLAG.

of this sign have also lived on in the northern
kingdom. At Borera, for instance, is a Celtic
cross, now overthrown; and whosoever wishes
for rain has but to raise this, according to
the local belief at one time, and he will obtain
his desire. It used also to be customary in

some parts of the country, when a bridegroom arrived at the church door ready for his wedding, to unfasten the shoe-string on his right foot and to draw a cross upon the doorpost. Such usages, however, seem to have been rarer in Scotland than in England.

St. Margaret of Scotland, a queen worthy of everlasting remembrance, who died in the year 1093, gave to one of the churches in her husband's dominions a splendid crucifix, on which was a figure of the Redeemer in pure gold. The one historic crucifix of the country, however, is the famous Black Rood of Scotland, round which gathers much both of legend and of history, and from which the royal palace and abbey in Edinburgh received its name of Holy Rood. The story of this ancient cross is recounted at length in the " Rites of Durham," and is as follows.

King David Bruce was hunting in a forest hard by Edinburgh one Holy Cross Day, or Feast of the Exaltation of the Cross (September 14th), and had become separated from his companions, when a wondrous hart, of great beauty and strength, suddenly appeared to him. The creature charged the king's horse, and so terrified it that it took to flight; but the hart followed "so fiercely and swiftly" that it bore down both the horse and its royal rider to the ground. Bruce, putting forth his hands to save himself, was about to seize the antlers of his assailant, when, from the head of the hart, "there most strangly slypped into the King's hands the said crosse most wonderously," and forthwith the animal vanished. On the following night Bruce was warned in his sleep to build an abbey at the spot where this miracle had happened. Accordingly, he sent to France and Flanders for workmen, built the abbey of the Holy Rood, which he gave to the canons regular of St. Augustine, and "placed the said Cross most sumptuously and richly in the said Abbey, ther to remayne in a most renowned monument." So it continued until "the said king" invaded England previous to the Battle of Neville's Cross; this sacred relic was then brought forth, and carried to the war. Again the king received a vision during his sleep, in which he was warned in no case to damage the patrimony of St. Cuthbert; but, in spite of this, he proceeded to lay waste and to destroy the domains of the great Abbey at Durham; and for this disobedience divine vengeance fell upon him. He

himself was captured at the ensuing fight, many
of the flower of his nobility fell on the field, his
royal standard became a prize to the English,
and the Holy Rood was taken! All the
trophies of the victory were solemnly offered
by the English as an act of thanksgiving at
St. Cuthbert's shrine at Durham, and the Rood
"was sett up most exactlie in the piller next
St. Cuthbert's shrine in the south alley of the
said Abbey." The writer of the " Rites " tells
us in one place that "no man knew certenly
what mettell or wood the said crosse was mayd
of;" at a later point in his story he implies
that it was of silver and was termed the " Black
Rude of Scotland" from "being, as yt weare,
smoked all over," doubtless from the tapers constantly burnt before it both in Edinburgh and
in Durham. At the Reformation this valuable
and historic cross was carried off with the
other abbey treasures, and no doubt found its
way into the melting pot.

Our chronicler is not quite sound in his
history. It was David I. who founded Holyrood Abbey, about the year 1128; and to whom,
therefore, the first part of the story relates; but
it was David II., son of Robert Bruce, and thus

a descendant of the first Scottish King of that name, who lost the relic at Neville's Cross in 1346. There is another story to the effect that St. Margaret brought the crucifix from the Holy Land in 1070; and that both religious and filial devotion thus prompted David I., the youngest of her sons, to raise and dedicate the abbey, which was to enshrine it. The saintly queen may perhaps have received the rood from Jerusalem, she can hardly have brought it thence herself, for it does not seem that she ever undertook that pilgrimage.

SEAL OF HOLYROOD ABBEY.

The seal of Holyrood Abbey, probably the most famous of all the many foundations dedicated in honour of the Holy Cross, contains a memorial of the legend above given. The centre is occupied by a crucifix beneath a canopy, with the Blessed Virgin and St. John on either side; below this is the Madonna enthroned and holding the Holy Child. A crosier, on one side of these figures, marks the dignity of the abbey; a stag, on the other side, with a cross rising from its forehead recalls the tradition of its inception; while the royal shield of Scotland below informs us of the sovereignty of the founder.

Bell Lore.

By England Howlett.

I N all Christian countries from the earliest ages the use of bells is practically as old as Christianity itself. The bell in its original form was nothing more or less than a piece of metal rolled into a wedge-like form and riveted together, and it is a curious instance of survival that the cattle bells in many countries are now practically of this primitive pattern. In the early days of Christianity small portable handbells were used for summoning the people to worship. It was not long, however, before the bell founder's art made great progress, and long before the year 1000 the music of bells pealing from church towers could not have been by any means a rare sound.

We must remember that although bells are primarily connected with matters ecclesiastical, still, more especially in the middle ages, they were used in all cases where it was necessary to give a public notice or warning. The commercial

34

transactions of a market were to a great extent regulated by bells. In case of fire or danger the bells were sounded to arouse or warn the people. In harvest time the gleaners' bell was rung to limit the time when the gleaners should set forth and return from their work. Before the days of the telegraph and quick travelling, bells were found to be a good medium for passing on intimation of any great national event or danger; and perhaps no sound has carried the news of such great joy and sorrow as the sound of the bell.

Gifts of bells to churches, particularly in the earlier ages, were always deemed the most acceptable of gifts, and during the middle ages these bells were not uncommonly given as a memorial of some deceased friend or relation. Kings and Queens may be found amongst the donors of bells, and one of the earliest royal bell givers was probably Canute, who presented a pair of bells to Winchester Cathedral in 1035.

The art of bell founding was principally, if not entirely, carried out under the direction of the ecclesiastics, prior to the thirteenth century. This, of course, is not to be wondered at when we remember that at this period the arts in

general owed their preservation and development
to the zeal and industry of the church.

In the early middle ages, not only in Scotland
but also in England and on the Continent, we
are told by Mr F. C. Eeles* that the richer
churches each possessed several bells, obtained
usually at various times, and often without regard
to their respective sizes, or to the relations
between their notes. The great bell was often
dedicated to the patron saint of the church, and
the smaller bells to the other saints who were
commemorated in the church below; each was
used separately for the services at the corresponding altar, while all were used for High Mass,
and on great occasions. A desire to ring the
bells in a musical way made itself felt very early.
On the continent this took the form of adding
a carillon to the already existing collection of
heavy bells, while here it showed itself in a
tendency to make the heavy bells themselves
form a part of the diatonic scale, and therefore
suitable for ringing in succession. Shortly before
the Reformation the carillon developed very
rapidly on the continent, and reached its perfection in the seventeenth century. It consisted of

* " Church and other Bells of Kincardineshire."

a large number of small light bells, fixed "dead," and sounded by hammers worked by wires from an arrangement of levers, something like the keys of an organ.

In Scotland, during the middle ages, the country churches as a rule had no tower. This was one of the architectural peculiarities of the country at this period, and as the use and appreciation of bells was steadily progressing at the time, we find the architects gradually adapting themselves to the requirements of the case. This they did, not by building towers as in England, but by elaborating a type of belfry which became almost peculiar to Scotland, a sort of architectural feature of the country. It is curious and interesting to notice that this type of belfry survived the destructive element of the Reformation, and lived on through the re-actionary period when art and taste were practically dead. Thus we often find in buildings otherwise devoid of all architectural pretensions, these redeeming little belfries which were evolved simply to meet the growing use of the bell.

Most of these belfries come under the head of the open stonework class, which, from their

very formation give an air of lightness and
freedom to the building they surmount. When
the Renaissance period came in the form of
the belfry was not altered, but the detail then
became of classical design.

In Scotland we find that in some of the
larger towns both the steeples and the bells are
the property of the municipality, the Church
only having the use of the bells on Sundays,
while on week days they are used by the town
authorities. The origin of this curious sort of
co-ownership would appear to lie in the fact
that in former times it was no uncommon thing
for a town to acquire a lien on the bells in
exchange for helping to build the steeple or
undertaking to keep it in order.*

The following extract from the Burgh Records † of Peebles exhibits a good instance of
this :—

" 1778, December 29. The Council in con-
junction with the heritors, agree to the proposition of building a new church, . . . The
town to be at the expense of building the
steeple and furnishing it with a clock and

---

* " Church and other Bells of Kincardineshire," Eeles.
† Chambers' " History of Peebles."

bells, for which it is to be the property of the burgh."

From the Perth Session Records, October 6, 1578, we find that "The Session ordains James Sym, uptaker of the casualities that intervenes in the kirk, to buy a tow to the little skellit bell—the which bell shall only be rung to the affairs of the kirk, also to the examinations, or to the assemblies."

The same Session Records for Perth, under date February 6, 1586, tells us that "The Session ordains Nicol Balmain to ring the curfew and workmen's bell in the morning and evening, the space of one quarter of an hour, at the times appointed—viz., four hours in the morning and eight at even."

In many primitive parts of Scotland, where there was no belfry, it seems to have been the custom to hang the solitary bell on a tree. A writer in 1679 protests against "that pitiful spectacle, bells hanging upon trees for want of bell houses." At Drumlithe the town bell used to hang on an ash tree, and thus continued to do until 1777, when a small steeple was provided for it.

Among the Church ornaments to be provided

by the parishioners in the fourteenth century
was "a bell to carry before the body of Christ
in the visitation of the sick." This was done in
order that all, according to the then teaching of
the Church, might be warned of its approach and
pay reverence to it.*

Saint John before the bread doth go, and poynting towards
    him
Doth show the same to be the Lambe that takes away our sinne,
On whome two clad in Angels' shape do sundrie flowres fling,
A number great of sacring Belles with pleasant sound do ringe.†

These hand-bells were also used in procession
on the Rogation days, and frequent notices of
them are to be found in Church inventories.

Small hand-bells were in general use in a
variety of ways in pre-Reformation times. At
the burial of the dead we find them used for
the double purpose of clearing the way for
the funeral procession, and also to call for
prayer for the deceased. The Bayeux Tapestry,
which was worked by Matilda, the Queen of
William the Conqueror, depicts the burial of
Edward the Confessor, and in this a boy
appears on each side of the bier carrying a

---

* " Bell Lore," North.

† Hope's Reprint "Popish Kingdome."

small bell. We find reference to the use of these hand-bells at funerals by Chaucer :—

> . . . . they heard a bell clink
> Before a corse was carried to the grave.

Hand-bells which were kept for this purpose were generally called "the corse bell" or "the lych bell," and by these names they are constantly found mentioned in Church inventories. The custom of ringing these small bells at funerals was sought to be stopped by the Bishops in the sixteenth century. In 1571, Grindal directs that "at burials no ringing of hand-bells," and a few years later (1583), Middleton directs "that the clerk nor his deputy do carry about the town a little bell called the Sainctes bell before the burial." *

It is a very prevalent belief that a large quantity of silver was used in the composition of the old bells, and that to this fact we owe much of the beauty and purity of their tone. It is commonly stated that in the middle ages it was the practice for our ancestors to throw in their silver tankards and spoons when the parish church bells were cast. However, a subsequent analysis of many bells of this period

* " Bell Lore," North.

which have since been recast show the proportion of silver in them to have been exceedingly small.

The ancient bells, when cast, were set apart for their sacred uses by a solemn benediction, often called, from a too close approximation to the office of Holy Baptism, the Baptism of Bells. The office and the ceremonies used, which can be found in the Pontificals of the Mediæval Church, varied very little after the ninth century. The bell itself was washed by the bishop with water, into which salt had been previously cast. After it had been dried by the attendants, the bishop next dipped the thumb of his right hand in the holy oil for the sick, and made the sign of the cross on the top of the bell; after which he again marked it both with the holy oil for the sick and with chrism, saying the words :—

"Sancti + ficetur, et conse + cretur, Domine, signumistud:
in nomine Pa + tris, et Fi + lii, et Spiritûs + sancti
in honorem Sancti N. pax tibi." *

It is interesting to notice that in many places the practice still remains of ringing the bells at particular hours when no service is to be

* "Bell Lore," North.

held. This is clearly a survival of the times when the bells were rung to call people to the mediæval services. We are reminded in "The Bells of Kincardineshire," * that at the present day various reasons, more or less utilitarian, have been given in Scotland for these old service bells. The country people say that the eight o'clock bell is to "let you ken it's the Sabbath," or to "gar the hill folk mak' theirsel ready or the kirk win in." This is very often called the "rousing bell," and the later bell the "dressing bell," or the "get ready."

The Perth Session Records, July 10, 1560, provide that "The Session, after the appointment of the order of communication, ordains that the first bell should be rung at four in the morning; the second at half five o'clock; the third at five. The second ministration, the first bell to be rung at half nine o'clock; the second at nine; the third at half ten." July 6, 1703, "The Session appoints that the church doors be opened at seven of the clock in the morning, and *not* till then; as also that the first bell be rung at eight of the clock; the second at half nine; and the third at nine."

* Eeles.

The ringing of bells at funerals is a custom
of ancient origin. It was a popular belief that
the sound of the bell had power to drive away
evil spirits. In England, Bishop Grandison of
Exeter in 1339 found it necessary to check the
long ringings at burials, on the grounds that
"they do no good to the departed, are an annoy-
ance to the living, and injurious to the fabrick
and the bells." *

Before the Reformation there were five bells
at Dundee on which "six score and nine straiks"
were given three times a day, to call to "matins,
mess, and even-sang."

Presbyterianism has naturally had a great influence on the bells in Scotland. Mr Eeles,
who is an authority on the subject, tells us that
the passing bell is no longer rung, nor is there
any ringing at burials beyond tolling the bell for
a few minutes as the procession approaches the
churchyard. In some parishes even this is said
to be fast dying out. In the Burgh Records of
Dundee "it is statute that an ony person cause
the gret bells to be rung for either saul, mass or
dirige, he sall pay forty pence to the Kirk werk."

The ringing of the death-knell was universal

* "Bells of Exeter Cathedral," p. 7.

after the Reformation, when it seemed to have
acquired a new meaning in the minds of the
people, having become degenerated, so to speak,
into a mere notice to the public that a death had
taken place. Shakespeare refers to this ringing
of the death-knell in his seventy-first sonnet :—

> No longer mourn for me when I am dead,
>   Than ye shall hear the surly, sullen bell
> Give warning to the world that I am fled
>   From this vile world, with vilest worms to dwell.

The Reformation and the decline of Gothic
architecture both combined to put their impress
upon bells. The Reformation naturally caused
a great change in the inscriptions, and the decline
of Gothic led to a poverty of design and an
abandonment of the fine lettering, crosses, and
other ornaments. Figures of angels and saints
no longer appeared, and soon the artistic black
letter gave place to the commonplace Roman
capitals. With these drastic changes much of
the romance of the bell has been swept away.

Saints and Holy Wells.

By Thomas Frost.

A MONG the results of the preaching of the Gospel to the ignorant and superstitious in the early ages of the Church there must, unfortunately, be included a considerable mixture of pagan beliefs and customs with the new religion, some of which have survived even to our own time. The sacred character ascribed to a great number of wells or springs both in England and Scotland may be traced back, in numerous instances, to pagan rites observed at them in pre-Christian ages. Some of these, as at Drumlanrig, in Dumfries county, and at Tully Beltane, in the Highlands of Perthshire, have near them a circle of stones, resembling those supposed to be associated with Druidism; and of the latter, Jamieson says in his " Scottish Dictionary,"—" On Beltane morning, superstitious people go to this well and drink of it, then they make a procession round it, as I am informed, nine times; after this, they, in like manner, go

round the temple," as he calls the circle of
upright stones.

In the little island in Loch Maree, in the
county of Ross, is a well or spring traditionally
associated with St. Maelrubha, who is said to
have been a monk of the monastery of Bangor,
in Ireland, and to have founded a church at
Applecross, in the same county, in 673. Pen-
nant, who visited Innis Maree in 1772, says :—
" In the midst is a circular dike of stones, . . .
I suspect the dike to have been originally
Druidical, and that the ancient superstition of
paganism had been taken up by the saint, as
the readiest method of making a conquest over
the minds of the inhabitants." The probability
of this appears from old Kirk Session records
of an annual custom in Applecross of sacrificing
a bull to " Mourie " on the saint's day. This
custom survived until the latter half of the
seventeenth century, when it was denounced as
idolatrous.

In the island of Lewis, one of the Hebrides,
are the ruins of a chapel formerly dedicated to
St. Mulvay, near which is a spring, the water of
which was supposed to be of singular efficacy
in curing diseases of the brain. The patient

was made to walk seven times round the ruins,
and was then sprinkled with water from the
spring.   In others of the Hebrides, and along
the west coast, there are many wells named after
St. Columba.   Almost every well in Scotland
is, indeed, named after some mediæval saint,
many of them of only local fame, and very few
having a place in the ecclesiastical kalendar.   St.
Ronan's Well, from the association with it of
Scott's novel of that name, is the best known
to the general reader.   It has been identified
with the mineral well at Innerleithen, in the
county of Peebles, which long enjoyed good
repute as a curative agent in diseases of the
eye and the skin, and also in dyspepsia.

The church of St. Fergus, in Buchan, com-
memorates an Irish missionary of the eighth
century, in whose memory a well in the parish
of Kirkmichael, in Banffshire, is named.   Concerning this spring, Dr Gregor, in his "Folk
Lore of the North-east of Scotland," says:—
"Easter Sunday and the first Sunday in May
were the principal Sundays for visiting it, and
many from the surrounding parishes, who were
affected with skin diseases or running sores,
came to drink of its water, and to wash in it.

The hour of arrival was twelve o'clock at night, and the drinking of the water and the washing of the diseased part took place before or at sunrise. A quantity of the water was carried home for future use. Pilgrimages were made up to the end of September, by which time the healing virtues of the water had become less. Such after-visits seem to have begun in later times."

The best known of several wells named after St. Helena, the mother of Constantine, is beside the road from Maybole to Ayr, and about two miles and a half from the former place. It used formerly to be much resorted to on the 1st of May, for the benefit of sickly children. St. Iten's Well, at Cambusnethan, in Lanarkshire, at one time was held in good repute as a cure for asthma and skin diseases. Martin, in a description of the Hebrides, written about 1695, mentions a well named after the same saint in the Isle of Eigg, which was regarded by the natives as a panacea for "all the ills that flesh is heir to." He gives a curious, and in view of the connection of holy wells with pagan beliefs and customs, an interesting account of the dedication of this well by a priest called Father Hugh.

"He obliged all the people to come to this

D

well," he says, "and then employed them to
bring together a great heap of stones at the head
of the spring by way of penance. This being
done, he said mass at the well, and then consecrated it; he gave each of the inhabitants a
piece of wax candle, which they lighted, and all
of them made the Dessil,—going round the well
sun-ways, the priest leading them; and from
that time it was accounted unlawful to boil any
meat with the water of this well."

St. Fillan's Well, at the foot of a green hill in
the parish of Comrie, was formerly much frequented on the 1st of May and the 1st of
August by persons in quest of health, who
walked or were carried three times round it,
from east to west, following the course of the
sun. This done, they drank of the water of the
spring, deposited a white stone on the saint's
cairn, and departed, leaving some rag of linen or
woollen as an offering.

Half-way between the bays of Portankill and
East Tarbet, on the coast of Wigtonshire, are
the ruins of St. Medan's chapel, within which are
three natural cavities in the rock, which at high
water are filled by the tide. Sickly children
used to be brought to the larger hole to be

bathed, and this is still done occasionally, though faith in such matters, as in so many others, seems to be lessening. Dr Trotter, who visited the place in 1870, had the ceremony described to him by an eye-witness as follows :—" The child was stripped naked, taken by one of the legs, and plunged head-foremost into the big well until completely submerged; it was then pulled out, and the part held on by was dipped in the middle well, and then the whole body was finished by washing the eyes in the smallest one, altogether very like the Achilles and Styx business, only much more thorough. An offering was then left in the old chapel, on a projecting stone inside the cave behind the west door, and the cure was complete."

There is nothing certain known about this St. Medan, though there are wonderful legends concerning her in the Aberdeen Breviary and elsewhere. Concerning the chapel in Wigtonshire, Dr Trotter thinks that "the well was the original institution; the cave a shelter or dwelling for the genius who discovered the miraculous virtues of the water, and his successors; and the chapel a later edition for the benefit of the clergy, who supplanted the old religion by grafting Christianity upon it; St. Medana being a still later institution."

St. Catherine's Well, at Liberton, near Edinburgh, has been regarded for centuries as a remedy for diseases of the skin, and is still frequented by persons suffering from them. It derives its name from a tradition, preserved by Boece, in his chronicle of Scotland, that the spring rose miraculously from a drop of oil brought from the tomb of St. Catherine of Alexandria on Mount Sinai, and this story was considered to be countenanced by the fact that drops of oil are often observable on the surface, a phenomenon now regarded as due to the decomposition of coal, or bituminous shale, in seams below. Boece says that Queen Margaret, the wife of Malcolm III., built a chapel near the spring, and dedicated it to St. Catherine; but this chapel, some remains of which were still standing at the close of the last century, was dedicated to St. Catherine of Sienna, not to her sister saint of Alexandria. Before the Reformation, the nuns made an annual visit to the well, three miles from their convent, in solemn procession, a ceremony due perhaps to the coincidence of name.

James IV. made an offering in this chapel in 1504, and when James VI. returned to Scotland in 1617, he visited the well, and, as Sir Daniel Wilson relates in his " Memorials of Edinburgh in the Olden Time," he " commanded it to be enclosed with an ornamental building, with a flight of steps to afford easy access to the healing waters ; but this was demolished by the soldiers of Cromwell, and the well now remains enclosed with plain stone-work, as it was partially repaired at the Restoration."

St. Bernard's Well, a sulphurous spring in the valley below Dean Bridge, Edinburgh, is traditionally associated with the sainted Abbot of Clairvaux. Its medicinal virtues appear to have escaped notice, however, until 1789, when the property on which it is situated came into the possession of Lord Gardenstone, who erected a handsome Grecian edifice over the spring, set up within it a statue of Hygeia, and appointed an attendant to dispense the water at a very trifling charge. The place then became a popular resort for the purpose of drinking the water, and in 1889 the statue of the Roman goddess, having become decayed, was replaced by one in marble, by the generosity of the late William Nelson, who also restored the temple and made the surroundings more attractive.

On Soutra Hill, the westernmost point of the Lammermoor range, there once stood a hospital founded by Malcolm IV., for the reception of poor travellers, and dedicated to the Trinity. Only a small portion of the building now remains, but near it is a spring known as Trinity Well, which in former times was much frequented on account of the healing virtues attributed to it. A similar reputation was enjoyed for a long time by St. Mungo's Well, on the west side of the hill named after that famous Scottish saint, in the parish of Huntley, Aberdeenshire.

There were springs also which were reputed to preserve from disease those who partook of their water. The virtues of St. Olav's Well, in the parish of Cruden, in Aberdeenshire, are recorded in the couplet—

> St. Olav's Well, low by the sea,
> Where pest nor plague shall never be.

Of St. Corbet's Well, on the top of the Touch Hills, in Stirlingshire, it was formerly believed that whoever drank its water before sunrise on the first Sunday in May was sure of another year of life, and crowds of persons resorted to the spot at that time, in the hope of thereby prolonging their lives.   Water for the font was often taken from holy wells, and it was believed in the middle ages that persons baptised with water from Trinity Well, at Gask, in Perthshire, would never be attacked by the plague.   Baptisms in St. Machar's Cathedral, Aberdeen, were at one time performed with water taken from the saint's spring ; and, before the Reformation, the font at Airth, in Stirlingshire, is said to have been supplied from a well dedicated to the mother of Christ, near Abbeyton bridge.

Passing over a number of springs with reputed medicinal properties, but not associated with any hagiological tradition, we find it stated by Mr J. R. Walker, in a communication to the Scottish Society of Antiquaries, that "many of the wells dedicated to 'Our Lady' and to St. Brigid, the Mary of Ireland, were famous for the cure of female sterility, which, in the days when a man's power and influence in the land depended on the number of his clan or tribe, was looked upon as a token of the divine displeasure, and was viewed by the unfortunate spouses with anxious apprehension, dread, doubt, jealousy and pain. Prayer and supplication were obviously the methods pursued by the devout for obtaining the coveted gift of fertility, looked upon, by females especially, as the most valuable of heavenly dispensations; and making pilgrimages to wells under the patronage of the mother of our Lord would naturally be one of the most common expedients."

Some saints' wells were believed to have the power of foretelling whether the patients on whose behalf they were invoked would recover, —a superstition which may be traced to Greek paganism of a time thousands of years before the Christian era. St. Andrew's Well, at Shadar, in the island of Lewis, was reputed to possess this power. A vessel filled with water from the spring was taken to the patient's abode, and a small wooden dish placed on the surface. If this turned towards the east, it was held to denote that the patient would recover; but if in the opposite direction that he would die. "I am inclined," says Mr Gomme, "to connect this with the vessel or cauldron so frequently occurring in Celtic tradition, and which Mr Nutt has marked as 'a part of the gear of the oldest Celtic divinities,' perhaps of divinities older than the Celts." The Virgin's Well, near the ancient church of Kilmorie, in Wigtonshire, was also reputed to possess this power. If the patient on behalf of whom the prophetic power of the well was sought would recover, the water flowed freely; but in the contrary case it failed to well up.

Votive offerings have been mentioned as made to the saints to whom wells were dedicated, and thus became holy. At Montblairie, in Banffshire, shreds of linen and woollen were hung on the bushes beside a consecrated well, and farthings and halfpence were thrown into the water. Miller, in his "Scenes and Legends of the North of Scotland," notices a similar custom as practised in the vicinity of Cromarty, his native town. He says, "It is not yet twenty years since a thorn, which formed a little canopy over the spring of St. Bennet, used to be covered anew every season with little pieces of rag, left on it as offerings to the saint by sick people who came to drink of the water."

St. Wallach's Bath, in Strathdeveron, is a cavity in the rock, about three feet in depth, into which water flows from a spring several yards higher up, the overflow trickling over the edge into the stream, about four feet below. Down to the beginning of the present century, large numbers of weakly children used to be brought to this bath to be strengthened by immersion in it, and some small article of the child's clothing was hung on a neighbouring tree. The spring was resorted to for the cure of sore eyes, and pins were offered to the Saint, being left in a hollow of a stone beside the well. At the end of May, which was the season for the visit, the hollow was often full of pins. Sir Arthur Mitchell, describing the holy well on Innis Maree in a communication to the Scottish Society of Antiquaries, says, "Near it stands an oak tree, which is studded with nails. To each of these was originally attached a piece of the clothing of some patient who had visited the spot. There are hundreds of nails, and one has still fastened to it a faded ribbon. Two bone buttons and two buckles we also found nailed to the tree. Countless pennies and halfpennies are driven edgeways into the wood." A more recent visitor, surprised at finding what appeared to be a silver coin fixed in the tree, took the trouble to examine it, and found it spurious.

Coins were more usually, however, thrown into the well, and Mr Patrick Dudgeon, who in 1870 had the well of St. Querdon, in Troqueer parish, Kirkcudbrightshire, cleaned out, observes in an article contributed to the transactions of the Dumfries and Galloway Natural History Society, that several hundreds of coins were found at the bottom—nearly all being the smallest copper coins, dating from the reign of Elizabeth to that of George III., but chiefly Scottish issues of James VI., Charles I., and Charles II. He mentions also having been told by old residents that they remembered seeing rags and ribbons hung on the bushes around the well.

Dr Macgeorge, describing St. Thenew's Well, in his "Old Glasgow," states, "It was shaded by an old tree, which drooped over the well, and which remained until the end of the last century. On this tree the devotees who frequented the well were accustomed to nail, as thank-offerings, small bits of tin-iron—probably manufactured for that purpose by a craftsman in the neighbourhood —representing the parts of the body supposed to have been cured by the virtues of the sacred spring, such as eyes, hands, feet, ears, and others."

Pilgrimages to saints' wells were a well-observed custom until they were, after the Reformation, prohibited both by the Church and Parliament. In an Act of 1581, allusion is made to the perverse inclination to superstition, "through which the dregs of idolatry yet remain in divers parts of the realm by using of pilgrimage to some chapels, wells, crosses, and such other monuments of idolatry, as also by observing of the festal days of the Saints sometime named their patrons in setting forth of bon-fires, singing of carols within and about kirks at certain seasons of the year." In accordance with this enactment, the Kirk Session of Falkirk, in 1628, ordered several persons who had made a pilgrimage to a holy well to appear in church on three appointed Sundays, clad in the garb of penitents. A warning was also issued that persons doing the like in future would be fined in addition to the penance, and in default, would be put in ward and fed on bread and water only for eight days.

In the following year, the Privy Council made an order "that commissioners cause diligent search at all such parts and places where this idolatrous superstition is used, and to take

and apprehend all such persons of what-
somever rank and quality whom they shall
deprehend going in pilgrimage to chapels and
wells, or whom they shall know themselves to
be guilty of that crime, and to commit them to
ward, until measures be adopted for their trial
and punishment." But though pilgrimages in
bodies were checked, individual visits to holy
wells continued. In 1630, the Kirk Session of
Aberdeen fined a woman for sending her child
to be washed in St. Fittack's Well, in the parish
of Nigg, on the opposite side of the Dee, and
she and her nurse were ordered to acknowledge
the offence before the session.

In course of time, such "offences" came to
be regarded more leniently. Fines gradually
ceased to be inflicted, and penance to be enjoined. In three cases entered in the Kirk
Session records of Airth, in Stirlingshire, in
1757, the persons cited were merely admonished.
But old customs have wonderful vitality, and
holy wells are still frequented. Sir Arthur
Mitchell remarks, in " The Past in the Present,"
that he has seen at least a dozen wells "which
have not ceased to be worshipped," though he
adds that the visitors are now comparatively

few.   Mr Campbell of Islay says, in his " Tales
of the West Highlands," " Holy healing wells
are common all over the Highlands, and people
still leave offerings of pins and nails and bits
of rag, though few would confess it.   There is
a well in Islay where I myself have, after
drinking, deposited copper caps amongst a
hoard of pins and buttons and similar gear
placed in chinks in the rocks."

Some of the wells once resorted to by great
numbers of persons have disappeared in consequence of changes of the surface.   The growth
of towns, railways, agricultural improvements,
have each had their part in the obliteration of
spots formerly deemed sacred.   The Pilgrims'
Well, at Aberdour, in Fifeshire, which for
centuries attracted crowds, is now filled up.
The like end has come to the Abbot's Well
at Urquhart, in Elginshire.   St. Mary's Well
at Whitekirk, in Haddingtonshire, has also
ceased to exist, the water having been drained
off.   Near Drumakill, in the parish of Drymen,
Dumbartonshire, there was once a famous spring
dedicated to St. Vildrin, and near it was a cross,
with a figure of the Saint upon it in relief.
Between thirty and forty years ago the cross

was broken up, and the fragments used in the construction of a farm-house ; and shortly afterwards the spring was drained into a stream.

There was formerly a holy well beside the lonely cross-road from Abbeyhill to Restalrig, near Edinburgh, and in the middle ages it attracted a great number of pilgrims. It appears to have been originally dedicated to the Holy Rood, but it afterwards became known as St. Margaret's Well, and Mr Walker thinks that the dedication may have been changed in connection with the translation of Queen Margaret's remains in 1251, on the occasion of her canonisation. There was a small Gothic building over the spring until the North British Railway Company acquired possession of the site and built a station upon it. The covering was then taken down, stone by stone, and rebuilt above St. David's spring, on the northern slope of Salisbury Crags. The water of St. Margaret's Well found another channel, and thus one more of Scotland's holy wells ceased to exist.

Life in the Pre=Reformation Cathedrals.

By A. H. Millar, F.S.A.Scot.

THE history of every Scottish city or burgh
of importance is intimately connected with
one of two possible originals. Each burgh has
taken its origin either from a feudal castle or from
a cathedral or abbey. This statement may seem
very sweeping in its character, but a close
examination will prove that it is founded on
fact. Edinburgh, for instance, grew up around
the ancient Castle—Eadwin's burh—while the
Cathedral of St. Giles and all the subordinate
churches were adjuncts of the secular centre.
The true ecclesiastical point of origin in Edinburgh was St. Margaret's Chapel, and it still
stands within the Castle walls. Glasgow, on the
other hand, took its origin from the Cathedral.
That building formed the nucleus of the original
city, and the first houses in Glasgow were the
Bishop's Castle beside the Cathedral, and the
dwellings and manses of the ecclesiastics in its
immediate vicinity. It was as a " Bishop's burgh,"

or community under ecclesiastical control, that Glasgow first had a corporate existence. The Bishop or Archbishop nominated the civic rulers, and though an attempt was made shortly after the Reformation to abrogate priestly control, and to transfer the power of the election of the Provost to the Guildry, the Protestant Archbishops strove to retain this right up till the early years of the seventeenth century. In 1639 the Town Council for the first time elected the Provost and Bailies, but even then the consent of the Duke of Lennox —who had received the secularised property of the Archbishopric—had to be obtained; and it was not until 1690 that the citizens of Glasgow obtained the right to choose municipal governors.

These two forms of origin may be traced in all the important Scottish burghs. Stirling found its centre in the Royal Castle; Dunfermline owed its existence to the Abbey. Perth originated from the ancient Church of St. John, and was long known as "Saint John's toun"; Inverness clustered around its baronial Castle. The Round Tower and the Cathedral of Brechin were the starting points of that burgh; and Paisley dates its history from the foundation of its Abbey. St. Andrews and Arbroath bear still unmistakable evidences of their ecclesiastical origin ; while Dundee found its first nucleus in its Castle, and after the destruction of that fortress the centre was shifted to the magnificent church of St. Mary, one of the largest parish churches in Scotland in the fifteenth century. It is clear, therefore, that life in the pre-Reformation Cathedrals and ecclesiastical buildings had an important in-fluence in forming and fashioning the history of the people. This fact is too frequently over-looked by modern historians.

Only two of the pre-Reformation Cathedrals in Scotland have survived unimpaired the icono-clastic zeal of the Reformers. St. Andrews Cathedral, the seat of the Primate of Scotland, was partially devastated by the Protestant mob, and weather and storm completed the ruin thus begun. Dunblane Cathedral has recently been restored and rescued from the wrecked condition in which it lay for centuries. The restoration of Brechin Cathedral is now (1898) in progress ; and the Cathedral of St. Giles, Edinburgh, has only been brought back to some of its pristine magnificence within the last quarter of a century. The two Cathedrals which escaped the fury of the Reformers are, the fanes dedicated to St.

Mungo (St. Kentigern) at Glasgow, and to St. Magnus at Kirkwall, Orkney. Both these Cathedrals had Episcopal Palaces adjoining the main structures, and from the history of these it might be possible to spell out the conditions of life during their palmy days. As Glasgow Cathedral shows in a remarkable manner the gradual development of a great commercial city from a small ecclesiastical burgh, and thus supplies a connecting link between remote times and the present day, it will be most convenient to treat it as a typical example of the far-reaching influence of early ecclesiastical modes of life.

Glasgow Cathedral occupies a very peculiar site. It is built on ground that slopes rapidly down from the level of the floor of the nave towards the bed of the Molendinar Burn. So steep is the declivity that a Lower Church— wrongly called the Crypt, but really an *Ecclesia Inferior*—is built under the floor of the Choir, only a few steps being necessary in passing from the Nave to the Choir, so as to give the requisite height to the roof of the "Laigh Kirk." Such a site would not have been chosen by a modern architect for a building of the same magnitude, because of the structural difficulties it presented ;

yet it has been asserted by Mr John Honeyman, an experienced architect who has made a special study of Glasgow Cathedral, that the whole design of this magnificent structure "was carefully thought out and settled before a stone was laid. It is a skilful and homogeneous design, which could only be produced by a man of exceptional ability and of great experience. Nothing has been left to chance or the sweet will of the co-operating craftsmen, but the one master-mind has dictated every moulding and every combination, and has left the impress of his genius upon it all." (" Book of Glasgow Cathedral," p. 274.) It is a remarkable fact that the name of this gifted architect is quite unknown, though a theory has been advanced that seeks to identify him with a certain John Morvo or Moray, a man of Scottish descent, born and trained in Paris, who was also architect of Melrose Abbey. But nothing absolutely certain is known as to the architect who planned Glasgow Cathedral ; and this is no unusual circumstance in the history of other ecclesiastical buildings. Referring to this fact Mr Gladstone once wrote thus :—" It has been observed as a circumstance full of meaning, that no man knows the names of the architects of our Cathedrals.

They left no record of themselves upon the fabrics, as if they would have nothing there that could suggest any other idea than the glory of God, to whom the edifices were devoted for perpetual and solemn worship ; nothing to mingle a meaner association with the profound sense of His presence ; or as if in the joy of having built Him a house there was no want left unfulfilled, no room for the question whether it is good for a man to live in posthumous renown."

Though the name of not one of the great architects who designed the Scottish Cathedrals has been preserved — unless we accept the doubtful theory as to John Morvo already mentioned — it is evident that the ecclesiastical designer must have been an important personage in every religious community from the beginning of the twelfth century until the Reformation. In those remote days it was not given to any architect to witness the completion of his design. That unique experience was reserved for Sir Christopher Wren, who superintended the building of St. Paul's Cathedral from its foundation till the last stone was laid. Many circumstances prevented the early architects from witnessing the end of their labours.

The poverty of the country, the perpetual war-
fare which ravaged Scotland, the impossibility
of employing the wandering Lodges of Masons
from the Continent so continuously as to ensure
the rapid execution of the work, and the frequent
changes in the Bishop or Archbishop who had
the control of the building, necessarily spread
the labour over centuries. Glasgow Cathedral
was begun by Bishop John Achaius during his
episcopate, which extended from 1115 to 1147.
It was not completed till the time of Archbishop Blacader, who died in 1508. During
these four centuries the original designs by the
nameless first architect must have been carefully
preserved, and handed down through a succession of equally unknown architects, until the
whole work was finished. Yet all these men,
whose brilliant ideas and excellent workmanship are at once the admiration and the despair
of modern architects, will ever remain anonymous. The Kings and Princes who contributed
towards the cost of the structure, the Bishops
who added various portions to the building at
long intervals, and the Archbishops who consecrated these additions are all carefully recorded ; but the architects from whose fertile

brains the ideas sprang, and the workmen who laboriously realised their dreams, are alike unknown.

The Cathedral of Glasgow took its origin from a *cella* erected on the bank of the Molendinar Burn, by the pious St. Kentigern. This early Christian Apostle was the natural son of Eugenius or Ewen III., King of Reged. His mother was Thanew, daughter of Loth, King of Lothian. Her name survives in a corrupted form as "St. Enoch," there being now several Scottish churches so designated, though she is distinctly denominated "St. Thanew" in pre-Reformation documents. The life of Kentigern is very fully detailed in the biography written by Jocelyn, a monk of Furness, at the request of Herbert, Bishop of Glasgow (died 1164), and is included in the "Lives of the Scottish Saints." The careful examination of this biography by Skene gives the probable date of Kentigern's birth as 518, his consecration as Bishop of Glasgow at 543; his foundation of Llanelwy (now St. Asaphs) in Wales at 553; his return to Glasgow at 581; and his death at 603. Kentigern was visited by St. Columba at Glasgow before 597, and his popular

name of St. Mungo (*mon gah* = my friend) was
then conferred upon him by Columba. From
the time of Kentigern's death until the twelfth
century nothing definite is known regarding
the history of Glasgow. Within the present
Cathedral the site of "St. Mungo's tomb" is
pointed out; and it is not improbable that the
magnificent pile was erected on this spot to
commemorate the founder of Glasgow. During
the bishopric of Kentigern it is not likely that
there was any building on the present site of
the Cathedral save the little *cella* or chapel of
the Bishop, and possibly a few of the houses
inhabited by the Culdee priests. It should be
remembered that the Culdees were not celibates,
but lived with their families in these rude
dwellings, which thus formed the nucleus of
modern Glasgow. When the ground beside
the Cathedral was turned into a grave-yard
every trace of these houses must have been
removed. It is possible that St. Kentigern
was buried within his chapel; and if so, the
tomb of St. Mungo, in the crypt of the Cathedral,
will mark the place where that primitive structure
stood.

The history of the See of Glasgow for five

The Duke's Lodging, Drygait.

D Small.

Bishop Cameron's Tower
Episcopal Palace of Glasgow

Town Residence of the
Rector of Renfrew

centuries after the death of St. Kentigern is almost a total blank; save for some dubious references to certain ecclesiastics supposed to have been the successors of the Saint, there is nothing to show the progress of the church in those days. The reforming zeal of Malcolm Canmore and Queen Margaret led to a revival of religion, as remarkable in its own way as the Protestant Reformation. The Culdees were supplanted by the Romanists, and the foundations were laid of a hierarchy that attained to vast power in Scotland. The reforms of the Queen were principally confined to the east coast—Dunfermline and St. Andrews—and it was not until her sixth and youngest son, David, Prince of Cumberland (afterwards David I.), ordered an "Inquisitio" as to the property belonging to the See of Glasgow in 1120, that any documentary evidence was made available on this point. Prince David had already procured the appointment of his chancellor and tutor John Eochey or Achaius to the bishopric of Glasgow, and with the installation of that prelate a new era began in the history of the city. The Inquisitio or Notitia showed that the lands possessed by the Bishop of Glasgow

were co-extensive with the kingdom of Strath-
clyde, and were in the upper ward of Lanarkshire, and the counties of Peebles, Roxburgh,
and Dumfries. Bishop John Achaius was consecrated in 1115; Prince David came to the
throne in 1124; and shortly after this accession
the Bishop began the building of the Cathedral,
which was dedicated to St. Kentigern on the
nones of July, 1136. Bishop John Achaius
died in 1147, and the Cathedral which he built
did not long survive him. It is probable that
it was a wooden structure, for it was destroyed
by fire in 1176, and in that year Bishop Jocelin
(1175-1199) began to rebuild it with stone.
The next "building Bishop" was William de
Bondington (1233-1258), who completed the
Lower Church (or Crypt) and the Choir. Bishop
William Lauder (1408-1425) began the erection
of the present tower, and partly built the
Chapter-house. These portions were completed
by his successor Bishop John Cameron (1426-
1446). Robert Blacader (1484-1508), the first
Archbishop of Glasgow, erected the crypt at
the south transept known as "Blacader's Aisle,"
built the splendid rood-screen and the stairs
leading from the Nave to the Choir and Lower

Church, and put the finishing touches to the Cathedral, which had thus taken nearly four hundred years to reach completion.

The gradual development of the Cathedral necessarily led to the increase of the ecclesiastics connected with it. The elaborate ceremonial of the Romish Church required a staff of officials far out-numbering that of the simple Culdee *cella* of St. Kentigern's time. No definite information is available as to the method adopted for supplying these officials in the early years of the Cathedral's existence. It is reasonable to suppose, however, that the Rectors and Parsons who had charges in the widely-scattered parishes under the control of the Bishop, would have stated periods when they would take their turns of officiating. These clergymen would likely reside temporarily in the Bishop's Palace, to which reference will be made presently. At a later date, as the grandeur of the Cathedral increased and its ceremonial became more ornate, houses were provided for them near the building, and thus a return was made to the social system of the Culdees, though with a celibate clergy. Even so recently as the middle of the present century, about twenty of the manses belonging to different prebends connected with the Cathedral could be identified in its immediate vicinity. It has been credibly conjectured that the remains of a building outside the north wall of the Cathedral mark the site of the Hall of the Vicars Choral, and a narrow lane between the Cathedral and the Bishop's Castle was known as the Vicar's Alley, probably because it gave access to the building. A consideration of some of these clerical homes will give an idea of the social life in a pre-Reformation Cathedral.

The Bishop's Castle was for centuries a central point around which the burghal and national life crystallised. The date of its erection is not known. The earliest reference to it is found in a charter of 1258, in which the Bishop alludes to *palacium suum quod est extra castrum Glasguense.* This phrase proves that in the middle of the thirteenth century there was not only a Castle in existence, but also a *palacium* or minor dwelling —not a " Palace" as the word has been absurdly translated, but a "place," equivalent to the old Scots word "ludging"—which stood outside the wall of the Castle. It is reasonable to suppose that Bishop Jocelin, who rebuilt the Cathedral with stone towards the close of the twelfth century, had caused the erection of the Castle to be begun, and that Bishop William de Bondington, who completed a large part of the Cathedral, also finished the Castle and the *palacium* referred to in his charter. The Castle would be constructed for defence in those lawless times as well as for residence, and would probably be a square keep surrounded by a moat. There was a Bishop's Garden in 1268, and the Bishop's Castle is mentioned in a document dated 1290. At the latter date Robert Wishart (1272-1316) was Bishop, and as he built rural mansions at Castellstarris (Carstairs) and Ancrum, it is probable that he extended the Castle at Glasgow beside the Cathedral. During the War of Independence this Castle became a stronghold coveted by both belligerents. In 1297 it was captured for Edward I., by Anthony Bek, the famous "fighting Bishop of Durham," and re-taken by Sir William Wallace. After Bishop Wishart's time references to additions made to the Castle are more distinct. Before the middle of the fifteenth century the moat had been partially replaced by a high wall. In 1438 Bishop John Cameron built "a great tower," at the south-western corner of this wall, and his arms with episcopal insignia were visible

on this tower in 1752. Archbishop James Beaton
(1508-1522) enlarged the tower and completed a
wall 15 feet high, which enclosed the grounds of
the Castle.   In the time of Archbishop Gavin
Dunbar (1524-1547) a gate-house or port was
erected on the line of the wall to form the main
entrance to the Castle.   From the fact that a
sculptured stone, still in existence, which was
taken from this port bears the arms of James
Houston, Sub-Dean of Glasgow, it has been
conjectured that the gate-way was erected at his
expense; and as he had workmen building the
Church of the B. V. M. and St Anne (now the
Tron Church) which he founded in 1530, he
probably employed them upon this other piece
of work at that date.   After the Reformation the
Bishop's Castle fell into disrepair.   It was partly
occupied by several of the Protestant Archbishops, but they had not incomes sufficient for
its up-keep, and after the abolition of episcopacy
by the Revolution of 1688 the Castle degenerated
into a prison for rebels and petty offenders.
Public executions took place in the Castle-yard
so late as 1784—a curious survival of the power
of the early Bishops over the lives of their
vassals, for it is said that the gallows of modern

times was erected on the site of the old "heading-stone" of former days. In 1755 the Magistrates gave permission to Robert Tennant to use the stones of the ruined Castle for the erection of the Saracen's Head Inn, a building which still exists though now divided into tenements.

During the stormy period of the sixteenth century, when Scotland was constantly in turmoil, through foes within and without the realm, the Bishop's Castle was frequently besieged. The legal proceedings that followed one of these incidents affords a glimpse of life within the Castle at that time. John Mure of Caldwell, acting under the orders of the Earl of Lennox, laid siege to the Castle on 20th February 1515, and captured it. He was soon compelled, by the Duke of Albany, to evacuate this stronghold, but before he retired his followers had sacked and pillaged the Castle. Two years afterwards Archbishop James Beaton claimed damages for the goods destroyed, and obtained a decree in his favour from the Lords of Council. The following articles were specially detailed in this decree, and are of interest as showing the furnishing and contents of an episcopal dwelling of that period : —" xiii feddir bedds furnist, price of ilka bedd

v marks ; xviii verdour bedds, price of the pere
xl⁵ ; xii buird claiths, xii tyn quarts, xii tyn pynts,
v dusane of peuder veschellis, tua kists, xv swyne,
iv dakyr of salt hyds, vi dusane of salmond, ane
last of salt herring, xii tunnes of wyne, ane
hingand chandlar, ane goun of scarlett lynit with
mertricks, vi barrels of gunpulder, ix gunnis, xiv
halberks, xiv steill bonnets, vi halberts, iv cross-
bowis, vi rufs and courtings of say, and iv of
lynning, with mony uther insight guds, claithing,
jewells, silkes, precius stanes, veschell, harness,
vittales, and uther guds." From this list it will
be seen that the luxuries of peace in which the
prelates indulged had to be defended by the
weapons of war.

While the Bishop's Castle was the centre of
ecclesiastical influence, the first extension of
Glasgow was due to the erection of manses for
the minor officials of the Cathedral. To any
one acquainted with the topography of Glasgow,
the city may be thus "skeletonised" to show
the manner of its evolution. The Cathedral
stands on an eminence rising gradually from the
north bank of the Clyde, and is distant about a
mile from the river. The main route from the
Cathedral to the Clyde is by an almost straight

succession of streets—High Street and Salt-market—which, unquestionably, follow the line of an ancient footpath. The origin of secular Glasgow was a small collection of huts inhabited by salmon-fishers on the bank of the river. A pathway was formed in course of time between this primitive village and the Cathedral, but for centuries there were no continuous buildings between these two points. In the time of Bishop Jocelin (1175-1199) the village had extended so far along the river-side and up the line of the present Saltmarket that the Bishop deemed it advisable to obtain from William the Lion the grant of a weekly market and an annual fair. About this time also, arrangements were made for the erection of manses for the ecclesiastics near the Cathedral. These houses were built on a road running at right angles with the foot-path to the river, the part going westward being called the Rottenrow (Ratoun Raw), while the eastward route was called the Drygait. There was thus a sacerdotal burgh in process of forma-tion on the summit of the hill beside the Cathedral, while a secular burgh was gradually developing on the bank of the river. In the course of centuries these two burghs were con-

joined, and thus the "backbone" of Glasgow
was formed. The ecclesiastical houses were,
of course, more elaborate than those used by
the fishermen and tradesmen who were soon
attracted to the place by the wealth of the
Cathedral; and thus it has happened that the
greatest commercial city in Scotland—the second
in the United Kingdom—took its rise from the
houses of the ecclesiastics by whom the burgh
was ruled for a very long period.

No record exists as to the time when the pre-
bendal manses were first erected, but it is certain
that Bishop Cameron (1426-1446) increased the
number of canons from twenty-five to thirty-two,
and caused all of them to build manses within the
burgh and near the Cathedral. The sites of many
of these manses can be identified from descriptions in old charters, and some of them have
only been removed within the past thirty years.
The Dean of the Cathedral, who was Parson of
Cadzow (now Hamilton), had his manse in the
Rottenrow. The Archdeacon of Glasgow was
Rector of Menar (now Peebles), and his house
stood in the Drygait. Long after the Reformation it came into the possession of the Duke
of Montrose, and was known as "the Duke's

lodging." It was removed about 1880, to make
way for an extension of the North Prison. The
Rector of Morebattle, Archdeacon of Teviotdale,
had a manse in the Kirkgait, now also absorbed
in the grounds of the North Prison. The Sub-
Dean was Rector of Monkland, and his house
was on the bank of the Molendinar Burn,
south-east of the Cathedral. The Chancellor,
Rector of Campsie, lived in the Drygait at the
place called "the Limmerfield" to which reference
is made in Scott's " Rob Roy." The Precentor
of the Cathedral, Rector of East Kilbride, had a
manse near the Castle, the approach being by the
Vicar's Alley. The Treasurer, Rector of Carn-
wath, also had a manse, though its site has not
been identified. The Sacristan of the Cathedral,
Rector of Cambuslang, lived in the Drygait, near
the house of the Archdeacon. The Bishop's
Vicar, Parson of Glasgow, had a manse beside
the Castle. The Sub-Precentor, Prebendary of
Ancrum, had a parsonage in the Vicar's Alley,
north of the Cathedral. The Parson of Eagles-
ham lived in the Drygait, beside the Archdeacon;
and the Rector of Cardross had his manse on
the south side of the same street. The manse of
the " Canon of Barlanark and Lord of Provan,"

in Castle Street, is the only remaining house supposed to have been occupied by him, though it seems more likely to have been erected after the Reformation. The Rector of Carstairs resided in a manse in Rottenrow, beside the houses of the Prebendary of Erskine and the Rector of Renfrew. Other officials who lived in the immediate vicinity of the Cathedral were the Rector of Govan, the Vicar of Kirkmahoe, Dumfriesshire, the Rector of Tarbolton, Ayrshire, the Rector of Killearn, Dumbartonshire, the Prebendary of Douglas, Lanarkshire, the Rector of Eddleston, Peeblesshire, the Rector of Stobo, Peeblesshire, and the Rector of Luss, Dumbartonshire. The houses of six of the Prebendaries— Durisdeer, Roxburgh, Ashkirk, Sanquhar, Cumnock, and Ayr—have not been identified, though it is extremely probable that they had to comply with Bishop Cameron's command, and to erect manses in the burgh. The Hall of the Vicars Choral, with accommodation for eighteen officials, was built on the north side of the Cathedral, by Bishop Andrew Muirhead (1455-1473).

From this list it will be seen how great must have been the influence of this Levite village upon the development of the burgh. The comparatively luxurious style of living among the ecclesiastics would attract craftsmen, artificers of various kinds, and merchants trading with other countries to supply the rich garments, the expensive wines, and the numerous delicacies which were deemed necessaries by ecclesiastical dignitaries of high degree. With the Reformation all this grandeur was swept away, but before that epoch Glasgow had been made the favourite residence of many of the Lowland noblemen; and when the sacerdotal burgh disappeared, the secular and commercial city was ready to take its place. The domination of the Church passed, but not before it had prepared the way for its successor. In other Cathedral cities in Scotland a similar process of development may be traced, though not in so distinct a manner as exhibited in the evolution of Glasgow. Verily, that city owes much of its prosperity to the foresight and patriotism of those who ruled in its pre-Reformation Cathedral!

Public Worship in Olden Times.

By Rev. Alexander Waters, M.A., B.D.

MANY changes in the form of Church service have been witnessed in the Church of Scotland since the Reformation. In the first book of discipline, compiled by Knox and others in 1560, it is stated that "to the churches where no ministers can be had presentlie must be appointed the most apt men that distinctly can read the common prayers and the Scriptures to exercise both themselves and the church till they grow to greater perfection." In accordance with this recommendation there were, in parishes where ministers could not be procured to preach and administer the sacraments, a class of men employed in the Church under the name of "readers," whose office was to read the Scriptures and a liturgy of printed prayers such as is used in the public service of the Church of England. After the Church became more fully plenished with ministers, readers were still in many places continued. In parishes supplied with both a reader and a minister there were two distinct services in the church on Sundays. There was, first of all, a preliminary service conducted by the reader. The service consisted of reading the public prayers and portions of Scripture. It usually lasted an hour, and when it ended the minister entered the church and conducted his service of extempore prayer and preaching. In the year 1580 the General Assembly declared that "the office of a reader is not an ordinary office in the Kirk of God;" and the following year it was expressly ordained that readers should not be appointed in any church. It is evident, however, that readers continued to be employed in the Church of Scotland long after that date, both during the episcopacy that subsisted from 1606 to 1637, and during the ascendency of Presbytery from 1637 to 1645.

The Westminster Assembly of Divines ignored the office of reader, and when the Westminster Directory for Public Worship was adopted by the Church of Scotland in 1645, it may be said that the service of the reader was ostensibly and almost practically brought to an end in Scotland. It has to be stated, however, that

readers were, nevertheless, employed in some
parishes long after their office had ceased to be
recognised in the constitutions of the church.
Mr More, in his account of Scotland in 1715, describes the Sunday service in Scottish churches
as follows :—" First the precentor, about half an
hour before the preacher comes, reads two or
three chapters to the congregation of what part
of Scripture he pleases, or as the minister gives
him directions. As soon as the preacher gets
into the pulpit the precentor leaves reading, and
sets a psalm-singing with the people, till the
minister by some sign orders him to give over.
The psalm over, the preacher begins confessing
sins and begging pardon . . . . then he goes to
sermon, delivered always by heart, and, therefore,
sometimes spoiled by battologies, little impertin-
ences, and incoherence."

The reader was usually also precentor, and it
will be a natural transition, therefore, to pass on
now to an account of that part of the Sunday
service which the precentor conducted. In the
Reformed Church of Scotland a very limited
space was originally allotted to the service of
praise in public worship. " There is perhaps no
country in Christendom," says Dr Cunningham,

"in which psalmody has been as little cultivated as in Scotland. Wherever the Church of Rome reared her altars, music grew up under her shadow, and gave a new charm to her sensuous services. But Presbytery gave little countenance to such a hand-maid." The use of instruments in the service of praise was repudiated or almost abjured. Organs were not even allowed standing room in church. In 1574 the Kirk Session of Aberdeen gave orders "that the organis with all expedition be removit out of the kirk and made profeit of to the use and support of the puir." On his visit to Scotland in 1617 King James endeavoured to inaugurate a more æsthetic and cultured form of worship in Scotland, after the manner of what he had seen in England. Among other innovations he set up an organ in the Chapel Royal at Holyrood. "Upon Satterday, the 17th May," says Calderwood, "the English service was begun in the Chapel Royal with singing of quirristers, surplices, and playing on organes." The popular feeling, however, that in 1637 was aroused against the service book was turned against the organ also, and among the outbreaks of 1638 Spalding records that "the glorious organes of the Chapell Royall were

maisterfullie broken doune, nor no service usit
thair bot the haill chaplains, choristis, and
musicians dischargeit, and the costlie organes
altogether destroyit and unusefull."

The old doctrine of the Church of Scotland in
regard to psalmody is tersely expressed in the
first book of discipline. " There be two sorts of
policie," it is said in that book ; " the one of these
sorts is utterlie necessary, as, that the word be
preached, the sacraments ministered, and common
prayers publicly made. The other sort of policy
is profitable, but not necessarie, as, that psalms
should be sung and certain places of Scripture read
when there is no sermon." And in accordance with
this doctrine there is very little singing of psalms
prescribed as part of public worship in either
Knox's Liturgy or the Westminster Directory.
In each of these manuals of worship there are
only two psalms appointed or supposed to be
sung during the minister's service—one before
the sermon and another before the benediction.
It is possible, however, that there was, from an
early period, a third psalm sung in the church by
the congregation, although that psalm was not
included in the service. Just as in modern
churches where instrumental music has been in-

troduced, there is a voluntary played on the organ during the time that the congregation are assembling, so in very ancient times, long before the Reformation, it was customary over a large part of Christendom for the people "to entertain the time with singing of psalms" till the congregation had gathered. And in Scotland within quite recent times the epithet of the "gathering psalm" was commonly applied to what is now called the first psalm.

Pasdoran states that, "It was the ancient practice of the Church of Scotland, as it is yet of some Reformed Churches abroad, for the minister or precentor to read over as much of the psalm in metre as was intended to be sung at once, and then the harmony and melody followed without interruption, and people did either learn to read or got most of the psalms by heart." What is here called the ancient practice of the Church of Scotland in the rendering of praise is just the practice that is observed at the present day. But soon after 1645 a different practice arose and continued long in the church. The Westminster Directory for Public Worship recommends that, "for the present, where many in the congregation cannot

read, it is convenient that the minister or some
other fit person appointed by him and the other
ruling elders, do read the psalm line by line
before the singing thereof." The practice was
accordingly introduced into the Church of Scotland soon after of giving out the psalms in
instalments of one line at a time, and so popular
did the practice become, and so essential a part
of revered use and wont, that very great difficulty
was found long afterwards in getting it discontinued. Indeed, the practice of reading the
line was pretty general until the beginning of
this century.

Loud objections were raised to the singing
of hymns and what, in Scotland, are commonly
called paraphrases ; and even within living
memory this innovation gave rise to bitter
controversy. Not a few persons maintained
that the only proper subjects for divine praise
in public worship are the metrical versions of
the Old Testament Psalms. But from the
date of the Reformation down to the sitting of
the Westminster Assembly, not only were
metrical versions of the psalms, but hymns
and doxologies also, generally sung in the
public worship of the church. The year 1650,

however, witnessed a change in that respect.
The present version of the psalms was that
year printed for use in public worship, and
no hymns nor paraphrases were appended.   It
was not until 1781 that a Committee appointed
by the General Assembly submitted " such a
collection of sacred poems as they thought
might be submitted to the judgment of the
church."   It is this 1781 collection of paraphrases that is still, after the lapse of more
than a hundred years, bound in Scottish Bibles
along with the metrical version of the Psalms
of David.   The paraphrases have established
a secure place in the psalmody of all the
Presbyterian Churches in Scotland.   But it
was not without contention and controversy,
strife and bitterness, that the paraphrases made
their way into use in the services of public
worship.   The writer has seen a worthy elder
violently close his Bible on the giving out of a
paraphrase, and remain seated while it was being
sung.

Having described the reader's and precentor's
service, there remains the service that specially
‚devolved on the minister.   It is well known
that a liturgy was at one time, and for a long

time, used in the Church of Scotland. Knox's
liturgy continued to be used by some ministers
and readers down to the year 1637 at least.
Its use was by no means universal, however,
during that period. Extempore prayers were
always popular with the general public, but
when young and raw readers, however sparely
gifted and not more than half-educated, took
on themselves, as they often did, to treat congregations to extempore prayers, the guardians
of public manners were shocked. It was a shame
to all religion, said King Charles I., to have
the majesty of God so barbarously spoken to;
and, as a remedy for this deformity, as he
termed it, in the public worship of the Church
of Scotland, Charles issued a new service book
to be used as a liturgy by all preachers and
readers. But neither minister nor people would
take the king's liturgy, and extempore prayers
became more established in use and favour than
ever.

It is well known that in Protestant churches
generally, and in the Church of Scotland particularly, the preaching of the word has always
been reckoned the chief part of the service of
the sanctuary. The quantity of preaching that

ministers had to give and people had to take in olden times was enormous. There were commonly two diets of worship on the Sabbath and very often what was termed a week-day sermon besides. It was customary for ministers to take up a subject or text and on that subject or text to preach for six or eight Sabbaths consecutively. It seems not to have been uncommon for ministers to take an hour to their sermon. And to keep preachers

PREACHER'S HOUR GLASS.

right in this matter, it was customary to set up a sand glass in the church.

It is doubtful if in olden times there was as much good order observed in church during divine service as there is now. In some of the old ecclesiastical records, we find curious regula-

tions for the preservation of order in church. In
the Kirk Session records of Perth we find an
instruction minuted that the kirk-officer "have
his red staff in the Kirk on the
Sabbath days wherewith to waken
sleepers and remove greeting bairns."
In 1593 complaint was made at Perth
of boys in time of preaching running
through the church clattering and
fighting.

The hours of church service on
Sundays were much earlier long ago
than they are now. In 1615 the
Kirk Session of Lasswade appointed
nine o'clock as the hour on which
service should begin in the summer
months, and half-past nine as the hour of service
in winter.

HOUR GLASS
STAND.

The neglect of public ordinances has at all
times been a subject of lamentation. In olden
days many devices are said to have been tried to
remedy or abate these evils. Those resorted to
by the Covenanters in Aberdeen in 1642 were
perhaps as ingenious as any that have ever
been adopted. "Our minister," says Spalding,
"teaches powerfullie and plainlie the word to the

gryte comfort of his auditores.   He takes strait
count of those who cumis not to the communion,
nor keepis not the kirk, callis out the absentis
out of pulpit, quhilk drew in sic a fair auditorie
that the seatis of the kirk was not abill to hold
thame, for remeid quhair of he causit big up ane
loft athwart the body of the kirk."

Mr Cant did not go quite so far, but being
annoyed that his afternoon diets were sparsely
attended, he naïvely dismissed his forenoon
audience without a benediction, and reserved his
blessing for those that returned to the second
sermon.

Church Music.

By Thomas Frost.

THOUGH the use of instrumental music in the services of the Church fell into disfavour after the Reformation, the existence of a sculptured representation of an organ in Melrose Abbey shows that instrument to have been known as early as the fourteenth century. That "regals," as they were then called, were placed in some of the principal churches, and used in worship, is also evidenced by documents still in existence. That these, however inferior they may have been to similar instruments of the present day, were carefully constructed, and at considerable cost, appears from the payments made to William Calderwood for "a pair of organs" for the Chapel Royal at Stirling in 1537, and for "a set of organs" for the King's Chapel at Holyrood in 1542. But the Reformation led to these instruments being everywhere discarded as partaking too much of Romanism to be acceptable to the followers of Knox.

The organs of the royal chapels kept their places for a time, but elsewhere the "kists of whistles," as they then came to be called, were broken up and the materials sold in aid of the fund for the poor. But no long time elapsed before the Earl of Mar, as captain of Stirling Castle, caused the organ in the Royal Chapel to be removed and broken up; and in 1571 the Scottish Parliament expressed approval of the act. The prevailing feeling against the organ was intensified when, in 1617, orders were given by James VI. that carved figures of the Apostles should be affixed to the seats of the choir in the Chapel at Holyrood, where the organ was then being repaired, after a long period of disuse and neglect. Instrumental music thus became associated in the public mind with what was regarded as idolatry, and so much excitement prevailed that the bishops advised that the restoration of the organ and the choir stalls should be delayed until it subsided.

In 1631 Charles issued an order for the erection of an organ in every cathedral and principal church, and thereby renewed the agitation against the instrument. The order was disregarded, and in 1638, when popular opposition to the introduc-

tion of the Anglican prayer-book was being
strongly manifested, the General Assembly ruled
that the attempt to introduce instrumental music
into the services of the Church should be resisted.
Spalding, speaking of the agitation of that period,
says that "the glorious organs of the Chapel
Royal were masterfully broken down, nor no
service used there, but the whole chaplains,
choristers, and musicians discharged, and the
costly organs altogether destroyed and unuseful."
Six years later, the General Assembly recorded
in their minutes the gladness with which that
body had received the news from their commissioners at Westminster of the taking down of
the great organs of St. Paul's Cathedral and
Westminster Abbey.

Psalmody was little more in favour than the
gilded pipes of the organ.   The Westminster
Directory for Public Worship, adopted by the
General Assembly in 1645, recommends that
"for the present, where many in the congregation cannot read, it is convenient that the
minister, or some other fit person appointed by
him and the other ruling officers, do read the
psalm, line by line, before the singing thereof."
Before this time, in 1642, there had been much

controversy in the western Lowlands concerning the singing of the doxology at the end of a psalm, a practice which was popularly regarded as a commandment of men, not to be accepted as a divine ordinance. The General Assembly, in 1643, took the matter into consideration, and ordered the dispute to be dropped. In 1649, however, the subject was again before the Assembly, which then resolved that the singing of the doxology should be discontinued.

In 1647, a committee was named by the General Assembly to examine and revise Rous's paraphrase of the Psalms, and Zachary Boyd was requested to make a metrical version of the other Biblical songs; but nothing was done in the latter direction, probably due to the desire for uniformity with the Presbyterian Church in England, and in 1650 the present metrical version was printed for use in public worship, without the addition of any hymns or paraphrases. Nothing further was done for the improvement of congregational singing for more than half a century.

The question of instrumental music was revived in 1687, by the erection in the Royal Chapel at Holyrood, by order of James II., of a large and magnificent organ, which was regarded as a step towards the introduction of the Romish service. So convinced were the people of this that the clergy of even the Episcopal churches discontinued the use of the organ in public worship. In the following year, when James had abdicated, and the fear of Popish devices had become allayed, the mob of Edinburgh testified to the national joy, and at the same time indulged their latent propensity to mischief by breaking down the organ and burning the materials.

As in England down to a much later period, so also in Scotland, a metrical version of the Psalms was alone in use in worship, though several attempts were made at different times in the last century to introduce hymns of a more distinctively Christian character, as well as more poetical than the old paraphrases of Hebrew psalmody. The matter was before the General Assembly in 1707, and again in 1742, when a committee was appointed to prepare some paraphrases of passages in the Bible, "to be joined with the Psalms of David, so as to enlarge the Psalmody." Three years afterwards, some examples of religious poetry were submitted by the committee for the judgment of the Assembly; but, as before, nothing was done, and the matter remained in abeyance until 1775, when it was suggested by the Synod of Glasgow and Ayr that the Assembly should take such measures as might be judged necessary to introduce the paraphrases of 1751 into the Psalter of the Church. These were, in consequence, again examined and revised by a committee, but it was not until 1781 that the committee made their report and the Assembly ordered copies of the collection (which had been printed in 1751) to be submitted to the Presbyteries. Pending the Presbyterial judgment, the Assembly allowed the collection to be used in public worship "where the minister finds it for edification."

The permission to use this collection of Biblical paraphrases was never recalled by the Assembly, but it has also never been made a permanent act. It appears to have been given reluctantly, and only as a measure of policy, in concession to popular feeling in favour of the collection; for it appears to have been previously used in several churches. "Use and wont," says Dr Edgar, in his "Old Church Life in Scotland," "have now given as valid an authority for the

singing of the paraphrases in church as a special
Act of Assembly could do. The paraphrases
have, on the strength of their own merits,
established a secure place in the psalmody of
all the Presbyterian churches in Scotland."

Instrumental music had, in the meantime,
continued to be banished from public worship.
The psalm to be sung was announced by the
minister, and the precentor, who occupied a
smaller pulpit below him, placed in a slit in
a lyre-shaped brass frame in front of him a card
bearing the name of the tune in large letters,
so as to be visible to all the congregation. The
minister then repeated the first two lines of the
verses to be sung, and the precentor struck his
tuning-fork on the desk. It was a custom of
long standing, probably dating from a time
when few of the congregation could read, for
the precentor to read and sing a line alternately,
which must, to persons unaccustomed to it, have
sounded strange, and certainly have destroyed
what little harmony there might have been if
the psalm had been sung differently.

It was not until the first decade of the present
century that the organ was called to the aid
of the volume of praise in the Scottish Church.

To Dr Ritchie, minister of St. Andrew's Church, Glasgow, belongs the honour of this innovation. With the approval of the congregation, he introduced an organ, which was played for the first time on the 23rd of August, 1807, not without producing a sensation and a protest. The Presbytery was convened, and the Lord Provost appeared before that grave body, at the head of a deputation of influential citizens, to protest against the minister's innovation on long established custom. The Presbytery ruled, "that the use of organs in the public worship of God is contrary to the law of the land, and to the law and constitution of our Established Church." The organ was summarily silenced, therefore, and the grand tones of that instrument were not again heard in accompaniment of sacred song in the Presbyterian churches of Scotland for more than twenty years.

The ineffective character of unaccompanied congregational singing was very slowly recognised. In 1829, however, the congregation of the Relief Church,* at Roxburgh Place, Edin-

* The Relief Church originated in 1752 in opposition to the system of patronage, and received its name from its relief from that burden. In 1847 it became, by union with the Secession Church, the United Presbyterian Church.

burgh, with the approval of their minister, had an organ erected in their place of worship. The act was clamorously opposed outside his own following, and the Relief Presbytery called upon the minister, John Johnston, to remove the offending instrument, under pain of deprivation. The response of minister and congregation to this command was the severance of their connection with the Synod. In 1845, a Congregational Church in Edinburgh set up an organ in their place of worship, and as each congregation in that denomination is an independent body, no outside opposition or interference was in that case possible.

The progress of the movement continued, however, to be very slow. A large proportion of the older men in the ministry still regarded instrumental music in churches as associated with Romanism, and when Dr Lee, the minister of the Old Greyfriars' Church, in Edinburgh, ventured, in 1863, to introduce a harmonium there, it was rumoured that he was a disguised Jesuit, seeking to Romanise the Reformed Church. He was well able to defend himself, however, and he did so with such ability and power that, in the following year, the General

Assembly ruled that "such innovations should be put down only when they interfered with the peace of the Church and the harmony of congregations." The cause was won. The Old Greyfriars' congregation subscribed four hundred and fifty pounds for an organ, which replaced the harmonium in 1865.

The Free Church lingered long in the rear of the movement, mainly owing to the opposition of Dr Begg, but in 1883 the General Assembly recorded a resolution similar to that adopted by the Assembly of the Established Church of Scotland in 1864, and opposition to instrumental music is now practically at an end. The prejudice against it still lingers, however, in some districts remote from the life and light of the larger towns. A story is told of a lady of the old school of religious thought, that, having been induced by some friends to attend an Episcopalian service, and being asked on her return how she liked the music, she replied, "It was verra fine, but waes me! yon's an awfu' way of spending the Sawbath."

Discipline in the Kirk.

By the Rev. Geo. S. Tyack, B.A.

IN no country and at no time has a more searching system of ecclesiastical discipline been attempted than in Scotland in the first century after the Reformation. Not only was the teaching or the practice of the unreformed faith punished with the severest penalties, not only was attendance at church and the learning of religion, as the reformers understood it, rigidly enforced ; but even the private life of the people was watched and scrutinized. The behaviour of the congregation on the way home from divine service, the amusements which formed the relaxation of the people, the dress of the women in the street as well as at kirk, the snuff-taking of the men, domestic broils and filial misbehaviour in the various households,— these and other such matters were discussed by ecclesiastical tribunals and visited with pains and penalties, as much as offences against human or divine laws. The country was overspread with

a network of church authorities claiming disciplinary powers, there was quite an arsenal of
punitive machines in every district, and the
whole system was kept in motion by the free
use of espionage. Verily, in Scotland "new
presbyter was," as Milton said, "but old priest
writ large," larger in fact than the original by
far. Even the soldiery of the Commonwealth,
sufficiently used to the methods of Puritanism
in England, were astonished and disgusted with
the ways and means of Scottish discipline; so
much so that during their stay in the country
in 1650 they destroyed many of the weapons of
this intolerable tyranny; and it is indeed surprising that the people themselves accepted it
so long with submission. That the Church has
authority to use discipline over its members is
admitted; and that at the present time this
authority is too little recognised is, in the
opinion of very many, equally true; but in the
day of its supremest power the Scottish Kirk
Sessions seem to have usurped a universal
authority. The punitive rights of the State,
the proper control which a man has within his
own house, even that discipline which every one
should learn to exercise over himself, all these,

as well as that influence which more strictly
is the province of the Church, the Kirk endeavoured to control and enforce by means of
its own ecclesiastical courts.

Of these courts the first was the " Exercise,"
as it was at first quaintly called, from the custom
of "making exercise," or critically examining a
given passage of Scripture; more properly
described as the Presbytery.   Next to this came
the authority of the Synod, or district court,
and the final appeal lay to the General Assembly.
Of these the higher courts not infrequently did
much more than exercise appellant jurisdiction,
issuing orders to spur on the zeal of the inferior
ones.

The methods of punishment employed by the
Kirk were various.   Excommunications were
freely launched against offenders, especially
against those who did not accept in their ful-
ness the teaching and practices of the reformers.
Public penance was also resorted to, often in
addition to some other form of punishment; the
penance usually involving the use of the " repentance-stool," or the jaggs, or jougs.   The
former of these was a wooden structure formed
in two tiers or steps, the lower of which, used

for less heinous offences, was named the "cock-
stool."   An offender, judged to perform a public
penance on this stool, was first clothed in an
appropriate habit, the Scottish representative of
the traditional white sheet, which consisted of
a cloak of coarse linen, known as the "harden
goun," the "harn goun," or the "sack goun."
Thus arrayed, he (or she) stood at the kirk

REPENTANCE STOOL, FROM OLD GREYFRIARS,
EDINBURGH.

door while the congregation assembled and
during the opening prayer of the service; just
before the sermon the penitent was led in by
the sexton and placed, according to the terms
of the sentence, either upon " the highest degree
of the penitent stuill " or upon " the cock-stool ";

where he stood barefoot and bare-headed during
the discourse, in which his sins and offences
were not forgotten. The congregation generally
wore their hats during the sermon.

The minutes and accounts of the Presbyteries
have frequent allusions to this stool and its
accompanying "goun." Thus at Perth mention
is made of the provision of both cock-stool and
repentance-stool, and in 1617 the Kirk Session
of the same place ordered a stool of stone to
be built. The Synods specially enjoined on all
parishes the procuring of a repentance - gown ;
in 1655 as much as £4, 4s. 6d. was spent in
one for Lesmahago, and in 1693 Kirkmichael,
Ayrshire, ordered one of a special fashion, "like
unto that which they have in Straitoun," to be
made. The repentance-stool has maintained its
place in scattered instances down to modern
times, one of the latest instances of its use
being in 1884, when a man stood on the stool
to be publicly rebuked in the Free Kirk at
Lochcarron. The Museum of the Society of
Antiquaries at Edinburgh contains the old repentance-stool, formerly used in the Old Greyfriars' Church of that city ; the repentance-gown
of Kinross parish is also preserved in the same

museum. It does not always follow that penance implies repentance, and the strong arm of the Scottish Kirk sometimes compelled a man to submit to the former without his experiencing the latter; such was evidently the case with three reprobates who were excommunicated in 1675 by the Kirk Session of Mauchline, Ayrshire, because of "their breaking the stool of

JOUGS FROM THE OLD CHURCH OF CLOVA, FORFARSHIRE.

repentance on which they had been sentenced to stand in presence of the congregation."

The jagg or jougs consisted of an iron collar fastened by a padlock, which hung from a chain secured in the church wall near the principal entrance. An offender sentenced to the jagg

was compelled to stand locked within this collar
for an hour or more before the morning service
on one or more Sundays. About the time of
the Revolution this dropt out of use, chiefly
from the fact that the State no longer suffered

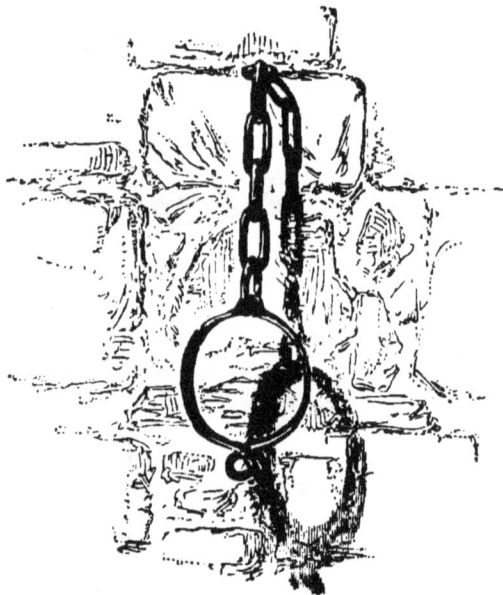

THE JOUGS AT DUDDINGSTON.

the powers of the Kirk to be carried with so
high a hand; several of the old jaggs, however, yet remain. At Merton, Berwickshire,
at Clova, in Forfarshire, and at Duddingston,
Midlothian, the instrument may still be seen
attached to the kirk wall; the jaggs of
Stirling and of Galashiels have also been

preserved, though removed from their original places.*

Besides the repentance-stool and the jagg, which were specially the weapons of the kirk, there were other instruments of punishment employed by the State, to which the Kirk also did not hesitate at times to have recourse. Just as the Spanish Inquisition handed over those whom it condemned to the "secular arm" for punishment, so the Scottish Kirk passed resolutions desiring the bailies to put this or that offender in gyves; magistrates were requested to imprison others, "their fude to be bread and watter;" employers were instructed to fine or chastise servants who used profane language; and town authorities were solicited to procure appliances for "ducking" certain classes of sinners. The brank or scold's bridle, the stocks, and the pillory, were used by the ecclesiastical, no less than by the civil, authorities; the Kirk also imposed fines, decreed banishment, used the steeples as prisons, and inflicted mutilation, and even death, upon offenders; its power

* For the accompanying illustrations of a repentance-stool, and of the jagg or jougs, I am indebted to Mr Wm. Andrews, from whose work on "Bygone Punishments" (London 1899) they are taken.

to enforce these sentences being largely due to the fact that civil disabilities followed the pronouncement of excommunication. The excommunicated person was an outlaw; he could hold no land, might be imprisoned by any magistrate to whom he was denounced, and was to be "boycotted" by friends, followers, and tradesmen; any one showing him the smallest consideration, or affording him the least assistance, was liable to a similar punishment. These large powers were only abrogated in 1690.

Among the offences dealt with by the Kirk, a prominent place was given to adherence to the unreformed faith, and to any apparent lack of zeal for presbyterianism. Saying mass according to the ancient rite, or even hearing it, or giving any countenance to such as did so, was severely dealt with. Hamilton, Archbishop of St. Andrews, was summoned, with nearly fifty others, before the High Court in 1563, charged with saying mass; and although he was liberated at that time, he was subsequently hanged. For a similar "crime," John Carvet was put in the pillory at Edinburgh, in 1565; other priests were banished in 1613; and another (John Ogilvie) was sentenced to be hanged, drawn and quartered in 1615. For hearing mass, John Logane was fined a thousand pounds in 1613, and many persons were from time to time imprisoned, or otherwise punished. The Church festivals were also put under a ban. The General Assembly in 1645 prohibited schoolmasters from granting a holiday at Christmas; the Kirk Session of St. Andrews punished several persons for keeping that festival in 1573; and in 1605 the same authority at Dundonald summoned a man for not ploughing on "Zuile day" (Yule). To harbour a priest, to possess books of Catholic devotion, to paint a crucifix, all these were recognised offences, which were visited with fines and imprisonment. In 1631 Sir John Ogilvy of Craig was committed to jail for "daily conversing" with supporters of the old faith.

The means adopted to promote reformed opinions among the people were equally drastic.

The most rigid observance of Sunday as a Sabbath was enforced. In 1627 nine millers at Stow, in Midlothian, had to do public penance and pay forty shillings for that "their milnes did gang on the Sabbath;" and in 1644 another miller, in Fifeshire, was sentenced to a fine of thirty shillings, with the same addition, for a similar offence. The uncertainty of the weather was not admitted as any excuse for Sunday harvesting, as is shown by a fine inflicted (together with the usual penance) upon one Alexander Russell and his servant for "leading corn on the Sabbath evening," at Wester Balry-mont. There are records of the stool of repentance being called into use for the correction of fishermen who mended their nets, of sundry people who gathered nuts, of a woman who "watered her kaill," and of another who "seethed bark," on a Sunday. The last named had to stand in the jagg for three Sundays as well. Lads who were found playing on Sunday were sometimes whipt, as in a case dealt with by the Kirk Session of St. Andrews in 1649, and others at Dunfermline in 1685. In 1664 it was enacted at Dumfries that "persons walking idly from house to house and gossipping on Sabbath" should be fined thirty shillings for their evil conduct; and in 1652 the Kirk Session of Stow actually compelled one William Howatson to do public penance for having, on a Sunday, "walked a short distance to see his seik mother."

But mere abstinence from work and play was

not sufficient; attendance at the kirk was compulsory. The amount of the fine exacted in
different districts varied, but everywhere even
a single absence was noted, and had to be paid
for. At Aberdeen, in 1568, the penalty was 6d.
for every service missed; at Lasswade, in 1615,
it was 6s. 8d. from a gentleman, and 3s. 4d.
from a servant; at Dunino, in 1643, the sum was
2s. for a first offence, 4s. for the second, and a
like proportion for others. Paupers who failed
in this duty were to be deprived of all relief,
by order of the Kirk Session of St. Andrews
in 1570.

The almost omniscient eyes of the Kirk
Sessions kept watch, moreover, on the behaviour
of the congregation while at the services. The
Kirk Session of Ayr summoned Andrew Garvine
before it and reproved him in 1606, because he
was late at kirk; and at Saltoun, in 1641, a fine
of 6s. 8d. was decreed against everyone who
ventured to "take snuff in tyme of divine service";
at Perth the Session's officer was instructed "to
have his red staff in the kirk on Sabbath days,
therewith to wauken sleepers, and to remove
greeting bairns forth of the kirk." The congregation was divided according to the sexes,

the men (most ungallantly) being allowed to
occupy forms, while the women sat upon the
floor ; and any departure from this arrangement
was gravely censured.   The dress of the women
also occupied the attention of the Sessions, their
habit of wearing their plaids about their heads
being especially condemned.   At St. Andrews,
the beadle was commanded to go about the kirk
during the service "with ane long rod to tak
down their plaidis" from the women's heads ;
while the authorities at Monifieth took very
extreme measures, ordering the expenditure of
five shillings in tar " to put upon the women that
held plaids about their heads."   Women condemned to do public penance upon the penitence-
stool were deprived of their plaids before ascend-
ing that ecclesiastical pillory.

The instruction which the people were to
receive was also regulated by the Kirk Sessions.
Before the morning service, and between that
and the afternoon service, the children were
publicly to recite their catechism, both for their
own edification and that of the people present.
So it was ordained at Stow in 1656, and at
Dunfermline in 1652, on the ground that it was
"usit in uthyre kirks."   But the passages of

Scripture to be treated by the preachers were also settled by the same authorities; the custom being, apparently, for the minister to go systematically through some complete book of the Bible. The Kirk Session of the "Kirk of the Canongait," Edinburgh, desired the minister, who had just entered upon the Book of Isaiah, "to begyne the Actes of the Apostles," after completing the first chapter of the prophet; and Mr George Gladstanes, at St. Andrews, was requested to take up the Second Book of Samuel. The length of the sermon was fixed also by the Session, as is illustrated by a resolution passed at Elgin, to the effect that Mr David Philips do "turn his glass when he preaches, and that the whole be finished within an hour."

All these regulations, moreover, did not apply exclusively to Sunday; for although the Kirk forbade the observance of old Church festivals, it rigidly enforced its own fasts and days of thanksgiving. There was public service in the towns usually every Wednesday and Friday, and work was as absolutely forbidden during service time on those days. and attendance at kirk as strictly enjoined, as on Sundays. Moreover, the non-observance of an appointed fast was visited with a heavy fine.

For the further protection of the people from any teaching contrary to the received standard, the Press was carefully guarded, and the publication of any work bearing on religion forbidden, unless it had first received the *imprimatur* of the Kirk's official "superintendent"; and publishers who issued books which proved to be obnoxious to the ecclesiastical authorities were compelled to withdraw them. The purchase of Bibles, moreover, was not left to the zeal or discretion of the people; but by an act of 1576, every householder worth 300 marks annual rent, and every yeoman or burgess having stock valued at £500, was compelled to procure a Bible and a Psalm-book, under a penalty of £10 (Scots).

Next to importance in the guidance of religious teaching and worship, and indeed closely connected with it, in the estimation of the Scottish ecclesiastical courts, came the question of witchcraft and sorcery. The annals of the country throughout the seventeenth century, together with the closing years of the preceding one, are full of stories of the trial, torture, and punishment of alleged witches ; and even in the early years of the eighteenth century there are occasional instances of persons proceeded against in the Kirk Sessions for using charms, and similar superstitious practices. The unfortunate women charged with selling their souls to Satan in exchange for occult powers seldom succeeded in establishing their innocence, and juries which ventured to acquit them were themselves occasionally charged with " wilful error " for so doing. Under these circumstances it would seem that the accused, abandoning all hope of escape, frequently took pleasure in exciting the wonder and the horror of the court by the weird and marvellous tales which they invented of their evil deeds ; and no tale could be too marvellous for belief. It made no difference in the enormity of the crime whether the supernatural powers ascribed to the prisoner were used for good objects or for evil ; Isabel Haldane, who " cured Andrew Duncan's bairn, by bringing water from the burn at Turret Port," Margaret Hornscleugh, who restored Alexander Mason's wife to health and renewed the milking powers of Robert Christie's cow, were burnt equally. with Agnes Simpson, who had raised a storm to drown King

James, and Catherine Campbell, who had struck her young mistress with convulsions. Foremost in hunting down these poor deluded, or maligned creatures, were the ministers of the Kirk; and practically the only lawful excuse for absence from a public service on Sunday, or even for the omission of the service altogether, was attendance at a witch-burning.

Much time of various Kirk Sessions was also occupied, now and again, in considering cases of pilgrimage to holy wells, "turning the riddle" to discover the name of a thief, and similar matters, and in reprimanding the offenders. So late as 1709, the Kirk Session of Kilmorie summoned before it a woman accused of "the horrid sin of the hellish art of riddle-turning," and sentenced her to public penance on three several Sundays.

More useful were the efforts, directed by the disciplinary authorities of the Kirk, to prevent such sins as drunkenness, profanity, slander, and sexual immorality. At Stirling, in 1612, a man was fined 20s. for being intoxicated; and Dunino had, in 1645, a regular scale of fines for such cases, 6s. for the first offence, 12s. for the second, and so forth. Cursing and swearing were openly punished at the market crosses, by the shame of the pillory, and by fines. Slander was met with the use of the brank, the pillory, compulsory shaving of the head, or, in extreme cases, with banishment from the district. In all these cases, a public reprimand on Sunday at the stool of repentance was usually inflicted, in addition to whatever other penalty there was imposed.

The violation of the marriage vow was made a capital crime in Scotland in 1563; but the death sentence was not actually carried out very frequently. At Glasgow, in 1586, it was considered sufficient to send the offenders to the pillory, barefoot and in sackcloth, and then to cart them through the town; but in 1643, the punishment was made more severe—the jagg, a public whipping, committal to the common jail, and, finally, expulsion from the town, being the satisfaction demanded by local justice. In the case of a minister who had admitted that he was guilty of adultery, the utmost humiliation was demanded. He had first to prostrate himself before the General Assembly, and implore their pardon in the most abject manner; he was then required to do public penance in sackcloth at the kirk door, and on the repentance-stool for two Sundays each, in three several towns, which

were chosen so as to complete his degradation.
Edinburgh, the capital, Dundee, his native town,
and Jedburgh, the place of his ministry, were
all to witness his shame. For other sins of
impurity, fines, imprisonment in the kirk steeple,
standing in irons at the market cross, and having the head shaved, were, one or more of them,
adjudged.

Some of the cases in which the Kirk exercised
its discipline were such as, it would appear to us,
might have been dealt with more effectually in
less formal or more private ways. When a lad
failed in proper respect to his father, like the
Glasgow youth who did not "lift his bonnet"
on meeting him, or even like him of St. Andrews,
who struck his parent, it would hardly seem
to have been needful to report the matter to
the Kirk, for it to deal with it; yet the Sessions
at those places solemnly considered these mis-
demeanours, in 1598 and in 1574 respectively.
Again, few husbands, now, would probably care
so far to confess themselves unable to control
their wives as to call in the authority of the Kirk
to prevent the "weaker vessels" from abusing
their lords; yet such cases frequently occupied
the attention of Kirk Sessions. The brank, or

imprisonment, or the pillory, was the sentence usually pronounced on these rebellious wives.

The interference of the Kirk Sessions in some matters, which they once claimed as within their sphere, would now certainly be resented. Thus, the presbytery of Glasgow forbade a marriage between James Armour and Helen Bar, in 1594, on the ground that the prospective bridegroom was " in greit debt "; and at St. Andrews, in 1579, all persons who could not recite the Creed, the Lord's Prayer, and the Commandments were debarred from matrimony. Moreover, the Kirk undertook the regulation of the wedding festivities. At Stirling, in 1599, the Kirk Session decreed that no marriage dinner or supper should cost above 5s. ; and this was an advance upon the rule passed at Glasgow, in 1583, which limited the cost to " eighteen pennies Scots." At Cambusnethan, in 1649, the presence of a piper at a wedding was forbidden ; and at Dumfries, in 1657, the number of guests was limited to twenty-four.

In too many instances the Kirk procured the information on which it acted in enforcing these decrees through spies of one kind or another. The informants, through whom cases were got up

against the adherents of the unreformed rites,
were often men of the worst characters, such as
Robert Drummond, a twice-convicted adulterer,
who finally died by his own hand.   The wretches
who hunted down and tested those accused of
witchcraft were scarcely more respectable agents.
Officers both of the kirks and of the municipalities
were required to watch for and report those who
did not attend divine service regularly; an
espionage of the most dangerous and objectionable kind being introduced when, as at Glasgow
in 1600, it was decreed that, on the "deacons" of
craft-gilds informing of any remissness in kirk-
attendance of their members, half the fine
imposed should be given to the gild.   Bailies
were desired to traverse the houses on "preaching
dayes" to see that the people did not stay at
home; beadles were "to tak notice of those who
tak ye sneising tobacco in tyme of divine service,
and to inform concerning them;" others were
appointed to take the names of such as were in
the alehouses after eight o'clock at night; mid-
wives and doctors were threatened with discipline
if they failed to report any illegitimate birth
which they attended; "searchers" were appointed to find out those who did not buy

Bibles and Psalm-books ; in a word the lives of the people were constantly under observation. It is perhaps the strongest proof of the strength of the Scotsman's character that, after a century or more of such interference with his responsibility, his sturdy independence survived. Much of this disciplinary system died away when, in 1690, it ceased to have behind it the civil disabilities attendant on excommunication.

Curiosities of Church Finance.

By the Rev. R. Wilkins Rees.

"THE plate for collections is inside the church, so that the whole congregation can give a guess at what you give. If it is something very stingy or very liberal, all Thrums knows of it within a few hours; indeed, this holds good of all the churches, especially, perhaps, of the Free one, which has been called the bawbee kirk, because so many half-pennies find their way into the plate. On Saturday nights the Thrums shops are besieged for coppers by housewives of all denominations, who would as soon think of dropping a threepenny bit into the plate as of giving nothing. Tammy Todd had a curious way of tipping his penny into the Auld Licht plate while still keeping his hand to his side. He did it much as a boy fires a marble, and there was quite a talk in the congregation the first time he missed. A devout plan was to carry your penny in your hand all the way to church, but to appear to take it out of your pocket on entering, and some plumped it down noisily like men paying their way. I believe old Snecky Hobart, who was a canty stock but obstinate, once dropped a penny into the plate and took out a half-penny as change; but the only untoward thing that happened to the plate was once when the lassie from the farm of Curly Bog capsized it in passing. Mr Dishart, who was always a ready man, introduced something into his sermon that day about women's dress, which everyone hoped Christy Lundy, the lassie in question, would remember."

This, from Mr J. M. Barrie's "Auld Licht Idylls," will ever be a classic passage on Scottish church finance, so far as it is represented by the collection. It is not, however, in such pages that the material for such an article as this must be sought, but rather in such fruitful fields as those afforded by, chiefly, the Kirk Session Records preserved in various parts of the country.

It has been pointed out, I think by Buckle in his "History of Civilisation in England," in comparing Spain and Scotland in point of superstition and religious intolerance, that the

latter country has denied to political what
it has conceded to priestly government, and
hence its superior material progress and prosperity. The general influence of the Kirk
Session, especially as exemplified in its disciplinary powers, was unquestionably large and
far - reaching, surpassing even that of magis-
terial authority. Hence we may find records of
fines levied by and paid to the Kirk Session
which we should have thought would have been
solely within civil jurisdiction. The church
revenue derived from fines must have been in
some instances quite considerable, and as
indicating their nature many entries derived
from old church records are of peculiar interest
and value. What the Church forbad *was* forbidden, and when her laws were broken or her
wishes not complied with, the culprit had to pay
the penalty. When the minister and the session
anathematized it was generally discovered that
it was not as with the Highland laird, who " did
not swear at anybody in particular : he jist
stood in tae middle o' tae road and swore at
lairge." The anathemas were directed at a
definite object, and of the luckless individual
thus aimed at it could not be said, as in the

"Ingoldsby Legends," "Nobody seemed one penny the worse."

The manner in which these fines were determined is sufficiently indicated by an extract from the Records of Session of Tyninghame, under date May 12, 1616:—"Maister Johne (the minister, by name John Lauder) heavilie compleinit yt ye last Lord's Day the Sabbothe was prophanit be sundrie pepill, as he was informit, by yoking thair cairts about 10 or 11 houris at evene, and led wair fra the see, to ye dishonour of God and evill example of utheris. For redress heirof in tyme coming, it is ordainit be the said Maister Johne and elderis present, that quhaevir sall yok to leid wair on ye Sabbothe, befor ane hour efter midnight, or until 12 houris at even be past, sall make publik satisfaction in the kirk, and pay 20s. *toties quoties;* and also ordains publik intimation heirof to be maid."

The following may be taken as supplying a commentary on this. It will, of course, be remembered that in the days here referred to Scots money was only one-twelfth part the value of what it is now:—"August 12 (1621).—The minister shew to the elderis that he had

causit wairn Robert Skugall, servitor to James
Neilsone, befor the session.   Callit on, compeirit, and accusit of carying netis to the
sea· in ane cairt, be yoking hors efter the
efternoone sermon, confessit the samin, bot did
it, as he alledgit, with his maister his directions.
James Neilsone, present, answerit yt he bade
him not yoke ane cairt, bot cary the netis on ane
horseback.   Ordainis the said Robert to satisfie
publicklie the nixt Lordis Day.   Item : Thomas
Airthe compleinit on ane man quha brocht salt
from the Panis to this towne this day, befor
sermon, to sell to qm presentlie the minister
past ; and George Shortus, the officer, with
him, arrestit the salt, and put it in Rot.
Quhyte his barn, that nain of it micht be sold
that day.   Takin fra him 12s. to the pure."
"August 26.—James Neilsone, accusit for com-
anding his man to pass to the sea with netis
in ane cairt, the said James denyit he comandit
him except only to carie them on horseback ; to
qm the minister answerit that the last day he
confessit he bade him yok the cairt, qlk some of·
the elderis·testifeit ; the brethren present ordainit
the said James to remove, to be censured, and
ordainis him to sit down on his kneis befor the

elderis and ask God forgiveness, and to pay twentie s. to the box, qlk bothe he did, and the session was qtentit."

Other extracts from the same records are worthy of note in this connection. On September 25, 1631, Alex. Jackson was ordered to give to the box what he received for the herrings which he brought in on the Sabbath day. He affirmed that he got but thirty shillings, which was produced before the session and put into the box. On April 3, 1642, John Nicolson was accused for hauling some lines in the water one Sabbath day, but the minister and elders, seeing him penitent, and submitting himself humbly, alleging that he did not get four shillings' worth of fish, ordered him to pay penalty, four shillings, and to make satisfaction on his knees before the session. The fishermen were, however, allowed to set their nets on Sunday, though not to haul them, as Dunbar records testify :—" 8 September 1639, Sunday.—Gude order keipit be the seamen at the draife; no herring brocht in, nor nets hauled, but only nets set at efternoon."
" 30 August 1635.—The session appoints some of the elders to go to the seaside at efternoon, to see that there be no mercat in herring ; and the

minister to be with them efter the efternoon, to
see guid order keepit."

Sabbath-breaking was, unquestionably, a fruitful source of church income. On December 26,
1619, it was shown to the minister that Robert
Barrie, hind to the Lady Bass, had thus offended
by carrying peat; and on February 4, 1621, the
said Lady Bass had to pay 18s. for a servant who
again broke the Sabbath. "Profanation of the
Sabbath," with its attendant fine, was again and
again reported. Sometimes it was football on the
links after the afternoon sermon, and drinking
after the pastime, which had to be atoned for by a
money payment, or again, it might be that "for
not being in the kirk in time in the afternoon"
the offender had to pay ten shillings, even
though he might have "come to the kirk shortly
after the third bell." Occasionally, it would seem,
the fines were imposed with drastic severity:—
January 21 (1644).—"James Kirkwood gave to
the session, to be put in the box, in name and
behalf of George Hay, in Scougall, tasker to
said James, 7s., because he came not with his
companie tymeouslie to the kirk that Lord's Day
his wyffe was buryed, as he aucht to have
done. . . . He said that the days were short,

and they had few to carry hir corpes, and the pepill did not conveine so tymeouslie as he expectit, and this was the caus."

Absence from worship caused many a shilling to fall into the coffers of the kirk. "Advertise them that they come to the kirk every Sabbath and that they that were convicted of absence, without lawful excuse, should pay six shillings every person, seeing they might now, the farthest of them, the days being long and the weather fair, come every day." This was in 1619. What a significant entry is the following :—" October 14, 1621.—The minister exhortit the peple to repentance. George Shortus searchit the towne." Or this :—"This day Alexander Davidson seairchit ye towne, and delatit some persons absent fra ye kirk in tyme of preiching." Absentees were followed and fined with an almost relentless pertinacity. Elders were ordered by the minister to search the town and " to delate the absentees." As soon as public worship began, the elder started on his quest, and the luckless delinquents were hunted in home and alehouse. A few days after, their names, with penalties attached, appeared in the session books. Sometimes no excuse was taken. An

elder, even though he pleaded headache as reason
for his absence, had to pay a fine; so had a
deacon with like adequate excuse; each exaction
tending to increase the income of the kirk.

But not only had Sabbath-day offences thus
to be acknowledged. On January 2, 1625, Alex.
Johnson, Patrick Wood, George Foster and
Patrick Bassenden were called on and accused
before the session "for troubling James Neilsone's house, singing at the door, being drunk."
The two former had to pay, "ilk ane of them,
3 lib. for thair dronkenness, if they be able, and
to seik the concurrence of the civile magistrat
for payment thairof; and if they suld refuse,
being unable, to speik the civile magistrat that
they micht be utherwayis punishit." And in the
same year it was found necessary to intimate
"out of the pulpitt, to absteine from drunkenes,
utherwayis if any suld be fund giltie thairof
suld be ordainit to pay thre punds." On
October 28, 1630, appeared an item of forty
shillings, Alex. Jackson's penalty for fighting,
"sent down by my Lord of Haddington to the
box, to be employed *ad pios usus.*" In 1659
the Kirk Session of Dunbar rebuked and fined
in £20 Scots a woman who had sinned when

Cromwell's army was in the neighbourhood eight years before! Such a sin-penalty was, as far as possible, applied to a secular purpose, and the *godly* poor were not supposed to benefit therefrom. In 1620 James Neilson complained of his wife's misbehaviour, and she was warned that should she disagree again she would be "inactit to pay 10 lib., *toties quoties*, and suld pay for this tyme also if she did disagree againe." And in 1642 "John Bryson's wife, in Scougall, is to be warned next day to the session for flyting with her husband, and abusing him by her unreverent speeches." The penalty for such speeches was "20s. *toties quoties*." Whether these ladies had private means, or the husbands had to endure the further hardship of providing the fine, history does not record. It should, however, be mentioned that cases sometimes occurred in which the fair sex were not to blame, as when a man was brought before the session for having assaulted his wife with a spade, and was fined a dollar, beside having to express his regret and to satisfy the session of his sincerity!

A few other curious sources of income may be mentioned. On May 29, 1625, it is reported in the Records of Session of Tyninghame that

"John Jakson was not to proceid in mariadge wt Helen Bassenden, bot that the mariadge was given over, and thairfor qfiscats to the use of the pure, and uther pious uses, the 40s. qsigned be him, according to the order maid thairanent." In the old Records of Innerwick, during 1608, it is stated that the minister having reported that the greatest part of the people were ignorant of the "Comands and very many of the Beliefs," the session ordained that if such knowledge were not acquired within a given time, a penalty should be paid; also that no marriage shall be "maid or parteis proclaimit until baith the parteis also recite ye Lord's Prayer, ye Belief, and ye Comands, or ells pay five libs. that they sall have them before the accomplishment of the mariage, qlk, if it be not done they sall forfeit." And in 1620, when a man excused himself for not having come to the examination, because he was ignorant, he was "ordained to heir the Word diligentlie and attentivelie, and to keip the examination; and in caise of absence againe, he suld mak publik satisfaction, and pay one merk."

The introduction of pews at the commence-ment of the eighteenth century was a means of obtaining additional revenue. As a return for the privilege of placing these seats in the previously open area of the kirk, "half-a-crown for the use of the poor," was demanded as a rent, and it was further required "that the same be payd before the seats be set up." The pew was also a source of indirect income, as when, in 1735, one John Porter was rebuked before the pulpit and heavily fined for pushing James Cobbam out of a seat in church, wringing his nose, and thumping him on the back. Bitter jealousy and anger were often occasioned by the pew, and hence free fights with accompanying fines not seldom occurred.

But the humours of the collection must not be altogether omitted. Burns, in giving his experience in "The Holy Fair," has immortalised the elder (Black Bonnet — so called from a peculiarly shaped black hat worn by him) who stood by the plate as the people passed into the kirk—

> "When by the plate we set our nose,
> Weel heapit up wi' ha'pence,
> A greedy glower Black Bonnet throws,
> And we maun draw our tippence."

And R. L. Stevenson refers to these elders, "sentinels over the brazen heap," when he says

of a countryman whom he met out West—" He
had a pursing of the mouth that might have
been envied by our elders of the Kirk. He
had just such a face as I have seen a dozen
times behind the plate." The elder, at any
rate, magnified his office and closely watched
each gift and giver. When a certain titled lady
once made a profound and formal bow only, in
passing, the elder followed her as she marched
in state towards her seat, and in tones distinct
enough to reach the whole congregation, said,
"Gie us less o' yer manners, my lady, and mair
o' yer siller." When in later days one of the
elders passed from pew to pew with out-
stretched ladle, he touched the people with it,
and with unmistakable directness would say,
"Wife, sittin' next the wee lassie there, mind
the puir," or "Lass, wi' the braw plaid, mind
the puir."

The obligations of the congregation in regard
to the collection were also frequently enforced
from the pulpit. Of "Wee Scotty o' the
Coogate Kirk" the following is related : "One
Sunday, when there was a great noise o' folk
gaun into their seats, Scotty got up in the
pu'pit and cried out, ' Oh that I could hear

the pennies birlin' in the plate at the door wi'
half the noise ye mak' wi' yer cheepin' shoon!
Oh that Paul had been here wi' a lang wooden
ladle, for yer coppers are strangers in a far
country, an' as for yer silver an' yer goold—let
us pray!'" And of Dr Dabster, "an unco bitter
body when there was a sma' collection," to
whom, before the sermon began, the beadle
used to hand a slip of paper with the amount
collected, we are told that one day when the
whole collection only reached two shillings and
ninepence, he stopped suddenly in his discourse
and said, with biting sarcasm, "It's the land o'
Canawn ye're thrang strivin' after; the land o'
Canawn, eh? Twa an' ninepence! Yes, ye're
sure to gang there! I think I see ye! Nae
doot ye think yersel's on the richt road for't.
Ask yer consciences an' see what *they'll* say.
Ask them an' see what they *wull* say. I'll tell
ye. Twa miserable shillin's an' ninepence is
puir passage money for sic a lang journey.
What! Twa an' ninepence! As well micht
a coo gang up a tree tail foremost, an' whustle
like a superannuated mavis as get to Canawn
for *that!*" After this we cannot wonder at
the old farmer's advice to the young minister,

"When ye get a kirk o' yer ain, dinna expeck big collections. Ye see, I was for twal' year an elder, and had to stand at the plate. I mind fine the first Sabbath after the Disruption, though our twa worthy ministers didna gang out, and the strange feelin' about me as I took my place at the plate for the first time. It was at ane o' the doors o' St Andrew's Parish Kirk, in Edinburgh. Noo, hoo muckle d'ye think I got that day?" "Oh, well, I know the church nicely," was the answer—"seated for at least two thousand—you might get two pounds." "Wad ye believ't?" responded the elder, "I only got five bawbees, stannin' i' the dracht for twenty minutes, too! If I had only kent, I wad rather hae pit in the collection mysel' an' covered up the plate. Mind, dinna expeck big collections."

The coins of other countries were strongly objected to. As far back as 1640, "The minister dischairget the people to give ill curreners," or the treasurer writes, "Collect 8s. 4d., whereof much ill cureners." And in the Records of Whitekirk, August 18, 1730, we find that "The minister and elders did receive from John Lermond, son to the deceased William Lermond, who was kirk-treasurer, the poor's box ; and the poor's money therein was compted, and there was in the box of good current money, at the present rates, ane hundred and ten pounds of whit-money. In turners there was of current coin 15lb., 10s. 10d. ; in Scots half merks, 12lb. ; in doyts and ill copper money, 2lb., 4s. 2d." This doyt ("not worth a doyt") was "a Dutch coin of debased metal, and equivalent in value to the twelfth part of a penny only." Its use in Scotland seems to have been confined solely to collection purposes. In Paul's "Past and Present in Aberdeenshire" is mentioned a rebuke once given by a Mr Wilkie, a minister of the parish of Fetteresso, whose income was chiefly obtained from the kirk-door collections. One Sunday morning he thus delivered himself : " When ye gang to Aberdeen to sell your butter, and your eggs, and your cheese, and get a bawbee that ye're dootfu' about, I'm tell't that ye'll gie't a toss up atween ye'r finger an' ye'r thoom, an' say, ' It's nae muckle worth, but it'll dae well eneuch for Wilkie.'" In the " Statistical Account of Scotland," the minister of Nairn expressively states that "the weekly collection at the church on Sundays amounted to about three shillings in *good* copper."

K

This spurious money often accumulated. Sometimes a box of such coins was given to the minister "to see what he could mak' of them" when in Edinburgh. "Sometimes," we are told, "a man would turn up in a district with a horse and cart, making offers for the bad copper or pewter that had been laid aside. At other times it would be sent to an open market, and there sold to the highest bidder. In 1774 there were over seven stones' weight of this truly 'filthy lucre' sold in the market-place of Keith, and its price was £2, 18s. 6d., less 4s. for carriage from Banff. . . . In order to counteract as far as possible the practice of putting spurious money into the plate, the various presbyteries under one synod used occasionally to combine and send as much as £100 sterling to the mint in London, and ask that the amount be exchanged for farthings, and returned with 'the first sure messenger.'"

But the use of the farthing has not been confined to the collections of bygone days. The Rev. John Russell, in his comparatively recent book, "Three Years in Shetland," thus writes of the collections in the parish of Whalsay: "The coin usually put into the ladle was a farthing. As the collections were exchanged at the shop for silver, and as it was at the shop where my hearers provided themselves with those farthings, I thought that if the Session hoarded up the farthings and so stopped the supply of them, we might get halfpence put into the ladle instead." This ingenious plan was not, however, put into practice, for the minister was assured that for the popular farthing would be substituted no gift at all. As to that perennial favourite, the bawbee or halfpenny, nothing need be said.

A few words must be given to the box that held the money—an important piece of Scottish ecclesiastical furniture that was jealously guarded. " Given to George Cuming, smith in Peffersyd, 32 pence for mending the lock of the box, and causing it to open and steek," is an entry under date, June 30, 1639. Innerwick looked well after the box :—" 23 April 1609.—The quilk day ye sessioune ordains George Wallace to keip the key of the box." But there are not a few entries in the Records of Dunbar which show that the box had been tampered with by the elder in charge; and for a considerable period one of the civil magistrates there took his place by the side of the elder at the plate on Sunday. The beadle also fell occasionally under suspicion, well merited at times, it is feared. In a certain Highland parish the money, after being counted, was placed in a box which was consigned to the care of the minister, who secreted it, with the key, in a part of the session-house press known only to himself and the beadle. Small sums were regularly extracted, and one Sunday when the minister discovered that the usual small amount had disappeared, he summoned the beadle. "David," said he, "there's something wrong here. Some one has been abstracting the church money from the box; and you know there is no one has access to it but you and myself." Thinking he had the beadle thoroughly cornered, the minister fixed him with his eye and paused for an answer. But David dumfounded the minister by this cool proposal: "Weel, minister, if there's a defeeshency, it's for you and me to make it up atween us, an' say naething about it!"

But if on the side of revenue we find much curious reading we find it none the less surely on the side of disbursements. When poor law and poor rate alike were unknown in Scotland

the Church took care of the poor, and that, oftentimes, in most thorough and effective fashion.
Even when other urgent claims asserted themselves the poor were by no means neglected.
A proclamation of the Privy Council, August
29, 1693, decreed that one-half the sums collected at the church door was to be given to
the poor as before, while the other half might
be retained for the relief of other distress, or
for any matters that might come under the
consideration of each individual Kirk Session
throughout the country. In the Kirk Session
Records of Falkirk, under date July 1696, it is
stated that "the number of the poor within
the parish church does daily abound," and the
session recommends to the minister " to intimate
to the congregation the next Lord's Day that
they would be pleased to consider ye present
strait and be more charitable." The response
to such appeals may not always have been
adequate, and in some records we find it stated
again and again that "the raininess of the day"
caused the collection to be so small that the
treasurer, instead of transferring it to the box,
handed it to the beadle.

The manner in which the poor were relieved is

sufficiently indicated by the following selected passages from the Kirk Session Records of Tyninghame, which, for our purpose, may here be considered typical :—

"November 2, 1617.—Given to ane pure honest man, quha had ane sair hand, 6s."

"May 23, 1619.—Given to ane pure man, lying sik in Patrik Jaksonis, being ane coupper in Tranent, 10s. His wyfe came befor ye session and earnestlie desyrit it, being in great necessitie."

"August 26, 1621.—Given to ane pure man, being ane scollar, 6s."

"January 26, 1623.—Collect 4s., given all to Thomas Harvie in Tyninghame, being ane ald honest man tailyeour."

"September 18, 1625.—To ane pure young man, being ane minister's son, 6s. 8d."

"September 7, 1628.—Given to ane stranger, being ane Transelvanian, 18s. He was supportit be all the kirks of the presbiteries."

"April 24, 1631.—Given to a man with a testimonial, robbed by pyratis, 9s."

"December 3, 1637.—Given to ane poore woman at the Knowis, callit the Daft Lady, 5s."

"September 5, 1641.—Given to ane poor scholar (being a minister's dochter), 5 dollars."

These extracts are also instructive :—"January 2, 1620. — Reportit that Andrew Law, being ane agit man grieve to ye Ladie Bass, was lying deidlie sik in ane hous. Ordainis to adverteis ane of the hostlairis to furnish him in drink and breid for a tyme, and out of ye box they suld gett payment, seing he was in great necessitie, being ane honest man. Ordainis also the Ladie to be adverteisit heirof." "January 30.—The said day given to them that furnishit drink to Andrew Law, being in great necessitie, 14s. 4d."

In the treasurers' books of the time, entries frequently occur of sums paid to "twa hirpling women, sairly needing something out of the box," or to "a lass wi' a cruikit back-bane," or to "a laddie wi' black een and a white face." Space will not permit any treatment of the interesting subject of badges for the poor.

One ludicrous incident in connection with a collection for the poor should be related. In Mr Sinclair's "Scenes and Stories of the North of Scotland" we read of a Highland minister who, notwithstanding an imperfect knowledge of the tongue, dared to make some announcements in Gaelic. He intimated that "on the following Lord's day there would be a collection for the poor of the congregation. But, alas, for him! he forgot how nearly alike in sound are the words 'bochd,' signifying poor, and 'boc,' which means a buck. The word he uttered was the latter

instead of the former, so that he startled his
audience by solemnly intimating a collection for
the bucks of the congregation!"

It seems that among the many and diverse
poor none needed help more sorely or frequently
than the schoolmaster. A flood of light is thrown
upon his condition by such extracts as these :—
" February 1, 1618.—The session ordainis that
Mr James Macqueine, schoolmaister, sal have of
everie baptisme 40d., and for everie mariadge
half ane merk—viz., for ye proclamation 40d.
and of ye mariadge 40d.—for his better help."
" March 8.—Ordainis ye wemenis penalties that
commits fornication to be given to Mr James
Macqueine, schoolmaister." " August 1, 1619.
—Given to Maister James Macqueine, schoolmaister, 4s., seing thar was verie few bairnis at
the school." " August 29.—The qlk day given
to Maister James Macqueine, schoolmaister, 24s.,
and 10s., being Cristen Stories penaltie, according
to contract maid with him." " September 26.—
Given to Maister James Macqueine, 25s., in
regaird of his povertie, and in respect he was to
go hame to ye Northe; in respect, also, of his
reading in the kirk." " October 17.—The quilk
day Mr James Macqueine, schoolmaister, desyrit

earnestlie some support, that he micht pass to ye Northe, seing thair was few or na bairns at the schoole. The session heirwith advysit. Ordainis thre lib. to be given to him."

"Maister James Macqueine's" successor suffered still more acutely from the eternal lack of pence. "October 22, 1620.—Given to George Davidsone, scholm^r·, for reiding and singing in the kirk, at his request, 40s." "November 19.—Lent to Mr George Davidsone, scholm^r·, out of the box, 18s." "July 15, 1621.—The said day George Foster his penaltie given to George Davidsone, schoolmaister and reiddar, becaus of his povertie." "September 16.— George Davidsone, schoolmaister, earnestlie desyrit somqt for his support out of the penalties, seing he had few bairnis in the school. Given to him 20s." "October 7.—Given to George Davidson 20s. of Thomas Greivis penaltie, the uther twentie given befor in respect of his reiding and singing in the kirk, he being verie puir, having ane familie." Soon the minister addresses plaintive appeals to the church in behalf of the said schoolmaster, and at last the climax comes. "December 1, 1622.—The minister earnestlie desyrit the elderis to have ane cair of George Davidsone, schoolmaister, now in great distress, being somqt distract in his witt, and desyrit that George Shortus, officer, wald cause some ane waik ilka nicht with him, and that the minister and he wald go from hous to hous for his support. The elderis promeisit to help, and to caus utheris to help." "December 8.—The minister desyrit bothe the elderis themselfs to help George Davidsone, and to caus utheris, he being almost now weill againe, seing he wald go over to Fyff againe. They promeisit to do the same. Maister Johne (the minister) reportit that he hyrit ane man on his owin expenss to go to Fyff for his father and brother to come to him—viz., Patrick Watson—and that he gave him 20s., and that his father has now come." "December 15.—The minister desyrit the elderis to help George Davidsone, being now well, praised be God! Given be the minister and elderis out of their purss, 45s." The schoolmaster's departure is, however, delayed, for in the following year, 1623, his name appears again. "March 9.—Given to George Davidson, 20 lib." "November 23.—This day collect at the kirk doore, for George Davidsone, being to depairt, 50s. 8d."

Assistance to cripples constituted a repeated charge on the church funds. "May 28, 1615.—Collect 4s., qlk was given to ane crepill." "Mairch 31, 1616.—Given to the belman for carrying ane puir cripple man off the toune, 6 lib." "June 21, 1618.—Given to Jhone Finla 3s. for carrying away ane crepill." "February 11, 1638.—Given to Alexander Storie, wricht, for ane pair of stelts to Henrie Caning, crepill, 4s." "September 23.—Four shillings given to carray away a crepill. We could get nane in the toune to carray away this crepill the morn, becaus of their business."

Payments for medical help were also frequently made. "May 28, 1615.—Gathered at the kirk door to give ane physician—viz., George Adamson, in Dunbar—for curing Agnes Tailzeour, in Peffersyd, 40s., qrof 28s. given to the pottingar, and the rest to the said Agnes Tailzeour, dauchter to Marion Peacock, in Peffersyde." "Januarii 3, 1641.—Given to Agnes Richisone (hir bairne being still vehementlie diseast, and hir husband at the camp), 20s. to buy cures." "Januarii 7, 1644.—Ane merk to Elspethe Duns sonne, lyklie to be crepill. 20 shillings given to his mother, to be given to the man wha

promeised to do diligence to cure the said ; to be
given for drogis." "July 20, 1645.—Given to
Robert Ewart, in Tyninghame, for curing James
Brown, his leg, 3 lib. 4s. 4d." All this links the
church finance of the Scotland of that day with
that of the early Christians, for in the *Apologia*
of Justin Martyr and of Tertullus we read that
the early Christians contributed or collected, on
the first day of the week, money for widows,
orphans, and others in distress, and particularly
for the relatives of poor slaves condemned to
work in the mines.

From the Kirk also was drawn much money
that eventually found its way into the pockets
of the sea-robbers of the Mediterranean. The
collections made at the church door largely
supplied the amounts necessary for effecting the
ransom of those luckless sailors who fell into the
clutches of the pirates. Hence we find :—" May
11, 1617.—Intimation maid to ye peple out of
pulpite to provyde something againe ye nixt
Sabbothe according to thair powar, for the re-
lieving of Jhone Mure, in Dunbar, and some
utheris, wha was takin be ye Turkis on the sea,
and deteinit be them in prison, seing thair was
ane collection to be maid throughout all ye kirks

in the qtrie to this effect." " May 18.—Collect at ye kirk doore for relief of them that wer takin be ye Turkis, 5 lib. 18s. 4d. ; the speciallis, or richest of ye peple, being absent, quhas portionis were also to be socht fra them ;" and " May 7, 1620.—Collect at the kirk doore for the Scottishmen lying in Algiers, taken by the Turkis, 3 lb. 17s. 4d."

Again and again we find in the pages of the Kirk Session Records reflections of the history of the time. Thus on December 5, 1641, " Intimation maid of collect the nixt Lord's day for ane pure honest woman, spous to umquhile James Freeman. He was slain in Ireland, and quarteret, as is allegit, for mainteining the Scottis Covenant." On February 29, 1622, " Earnest exhortations maid to the pepill anent ye contributions to the Kirk of God in France. Collect this day efter the sermon threttie pund, 8s. 2d. ;" and on March 3, " Qtribut this day at ye kirk door to the Kirk of France 3 punds, 11s. 10d." On August 28, 1646, a collection was made in the parish church of Auchterhouse for the people of Cullen, who had suffered much from the burning of their town by the Marquis of Montrose on his march northward ; and in 1746 the Falkirk beadle begged the Kirk Session to lend him five shillings because of harsh treatment he had endured at the hands of Prince Charlie's soldiers on their retreat from England.

Among the miscellanea of church finance as concerning expenditure the following should, undoubtedly, have place. The stool of repentance —imposing and certainly not cheap—deserves some prominence. "Given to Andrew Stone, wricht, 22s., and 2s. to his man, for mending and repairing the stoole of repentance;" and "David Nimmo, wricht in Lintoun, compeirit, and desyrit payment for making and repairing the stoole for repentance. The minister and elders herewith advysit; deliverit to him, out of the box, aucht pounds, and sax shillings to his sonne, and twentie s. to James Paterson, mason," are two suggestive items. Alexander Sherrie receives six shillings on April 19, 1635, "to buy poudder with to shett the dowes in the kirk, becaus they filet the seitts." At Cullen Parish Church, in the session records for 1703, the treasurer writes:—"For a calf's skinn to be a cover to ye Kirke bible, 7s. For dressing ye skinn bought to cover ye Kirke bible, and alm'd leither to fasten ye cover to ye brods, and for sowing thereof, 10s. For keepers to ye clasps, brass nails putting on ye stoods, and gluing loose leaves, 14s." Dr Russell, writing in his "Reminiscences of Yarrow," about his father's pastorate in the Vale of Ettrick, says, "At the first Martinmas of my father's incumbency, Robin (Robert Hogg, the father of the Ettrick Shepherd) came to him and said, 'Sir, Mr Potts (the predecessor of Dr Russell's father) used always to allow me five shillings of the collections in the kirk at this time, for gathering the bawbees, in order to buy a pair of shoon!' But to his disappointment, my father replied that he could not take it on him to make this application of the public money." The beadle, however, sometimes got the price of a pair of shoes; and in one book, in 1615, we have "*Nota* (a word scarcely ever used) That in all the gatherings for the poor there is the price of ane pint of ale, that collect which is set doun in the session-books, because of the pains which the clerk of the kirkmen taks in going thrice aboot the toune, and ance efternoon. This custom of giving sae mickle to the beadle has been ust of ald in this parish."

In February, 1733, a certain Jean Hall, a pauper in the parish of Morebattle, dies, and on

the 16th of the month James Robson, in Kirk
Yetholm, receives £3, 14s. 3d. for "cheese,
tobacco, and pipes" provided at the funeral.
"The digging of the grave, the crying of
deceased's effects at the roup, and the ringing of
the 'passing-bell' are all provided for by the
treasurer, out of his continually replenishing
and inexhaustible kirk-box." At one time thirty
shillings is given for a winding sheet for a "dead
corpse" which came in on the sands of Aldhame,
and, at another, twenty-five shillings is given for
one for a man "quha came in Peffersand and was
buryed the last week." Sometimes twelve shillings
is given to a man for reading and singing at the
communion, and, occasionally, as much as twenty
pounds is given to buy a horse, "seing he had
ane horse deid latly, and fallen abak in meins;"
or there is given out of the penalties to Alexander
Sherrie, "for mending and translating the pulpitt,
ane dollar." (In the writer's article, "Witchcraft and the Kirk," in the present volume,
reference is made to expenditure occasioned by
the imprisonment and execution of witches.)

Help is given to Dundee for a new harbour,
to North Esk for a bridge, and to Glasgow because of a disastrous fire. Even "a collection

for the Northern Infirmity" is mentioned, but this
is an obvious reference to the Northern Infirmary.

One closing quotation must suffice :—" May 2.
—The minister also shew to the elderis that the
bishop, at the last Provinciall Assemblie, haldin
at Edinburghe, the twentie of April 1619, ordainis
everie minister to bring ye contribution for ye
students of ye new colledge in Saint Androis,
and everie minister to give it to ye moderator of
the presbiterie quhair he dwellis, that it micht be
sent to Saint Androis. The minister shew to
ye elderis that ye kirk of Tyninghame was
ordainit to pay thre lib. yerlie. The elderis wer
unwilling to grant thairto. The minister shew
them that everie kirk was appointit to pay, and
that he wald give 20s. out of his awin purse to
that effect, seing thair was little in the box, and
many puir in the parishe. They grantit thairto,
bot with some regraits." " May 9.—The said
day takin out of the box 34s., and 6s. of Jhone
Walker's penaltie ; and Maister Jhone (the
minister) gave 20s. out of his awin purse to make
out thre lib. to be given for ye qtribution to ye
studentis in the new colledge at St. Androis." This
is but one among many contributions made by the
minister to fulfil obligations resting on the kirk.

Witchcraft and the Kirk.

BY THE REV. R. WILKINS REES.

FOR centuries belief in witchcraft was an article of faith with dour and brooding Scots. The Scot was made by Scotland; the country stamped an indelible impress on every characteristic of its inhabitants. With much truth it has been said, "From the cradle to the grave the Scotch peasant went his way attended by the phantoms of this mysterious world; always recognising its warnings, always seeing the shadows which it cast of coming events, and so burdening himself with a weight of grim and eëry superstition, that we marvel he did not stumble and grow faint, seeing that his dreary Calvinistic creed could have brought him little hope or comfort. Nay, it is a question whether his superstition did not partly grow out of, or was fostered by, his hard, cold religion. Superstition is the shadow of Religion, and from the shadow we may infer the nature of the substance or object that casts it."

There are traditions concerning witchcraft, even earlier than that of the fourth century which credits his Satanic Majesty with such a hatred of St. Patrick's sterling piety that he roused the whole tribe of witches against him. St. Patrick fled from the determined assault, and finding, near the mouth of the Clyde, a boat, set off in haste for Ireland. But running water being ever an insuperable barrier in the path of a witch's progress, these emissaries of Satan tore up a huge rock and hurled it after the departing saint. With the proverbial inaccuracy of feminine aim they missed their mark, but the mass itself ultimately became the fortress of Dumbarton. In those early days the marvels of witchcraft were great and many—Holinshed, among others, has chronicled the same—and, at the close of the seventh century, King Kenneth, fearful of his own safety and the stability of his throne, decreed that jugglers, wizards, necromancers, and such as call up spirits, "and use to seek upon them for helpe, let them be burnt to death."

That persons accused of witchcraft suffered death is unquestionably true, as in the cases of the Earl of Mar in 1479, and Lady Janet

Douglas in 1537, the executions of whom are foul blots on the pages of history. But it can hardly be said that it was witchcraft as an offence against religion or as mere superstition that was so punished. It was rather witchcraft in its political bearings—generally, in fact, as connected with treason and not with sorcery—that received condemnation.

But with the advent of Calvinism—the natural turn of the Scottish nation for metaphysical discussion induced them to receive the doctrines of the Reformation with general interest and favour—it would seem that the "crime" of witchcraft was looked upon in a somewhat different light. In 1563 the Scottish Parliament by statute, for which John Knox was a chief agitator, formally constituted witchcraft and dealing with witches a capital offence. "That all who used witchcraft, sorcery, necromancy, or pretended skill therein, and all consulters of witches and sorcerers, should be punished capitally" (Erskine's "Institutes," p. 706). And henceforth the irreligion of witchcraft caused it to be regarded as an offence against the law of the country, and the Kirk and its connections played an important part in the stern measures adopted for its suppression, doing their work with resolute determination and fanatical zeal. The authority of the ministry was great; its influence preponderated. Its friends were the allies, its opponents the enemies, of heaven. The theocracy which the clergy asserted on behalf of the Kirk was not so distinctly understood, or so prudently regulated, but that its administrators too often interfered with the civil rule. Old Mellvin's words were suggestive of much when, grasping King James the Sixth's sleeve, he told him that in Scotland there were two kingdoms—that in which he was acknowledged monarch, and that in which kings and nobles were but God's silly vassals ; and the clergy were but too apt to assert the superiority of the latter, which was visibly governed by the assembly of the Kirk in the name of their unseen and omnipotent Head. To disobey the king might be high treason, but to disobey the kirk, acting in the name of the Deity, was a yet deeper crime, and was to be feared as incurring the wrath which is fatal both to body and soul. With severity the Presbyterian teachers inflicted church penances, and with rigour they assumed dominion over the laity in all cases in which religion could be possibly alleged as a motive or pretext, that is to say, in almost all cases whatever.

Led by their clergy, and believing fully as they did in the literal interpretation of all Biblical imagery and the personal appearances of the devil, the people of Scotland waged a fierce unresting war against a great number of ill-fated individuals, whose only ground for being attacked was some physical or mental peculiarity, or who suffered simply because of the malice or ignorance of their accusers. At one time, stupid justices, instigated by foolish clergymen, consigned to torture and the stake almost every old woman dragged before them, even though brought only by the spite of malicious neighbours. In his preface to the *Bibliotheque de Carabas* edition of Robert Kirk's "Secret Commonwealth of Elves, Fauns, and Fairies," Mr Andrew Lang says: "Some of the witches who suffered at Presbyterian hands were merely narrators of popular tales about the state of the dead. That she trafficked with the dead, and from a ghost won a medical recipe for the cure of Archbishop Adamson of St. Andrews, was the charge against Alison Pearson. . . . 'She was execut in Edinbruche for a witch.'" On several occasions, commissions were issued by King James for the purpose of "haulding Justice Courtis on Witches and Sorceraris." The commissioners gave warrants in their turn to the minister and elders of each parish in the shire to examine suspected parties and to frame an indictment against them. And as a rule the accused were overwhelmed by a huge heap of rumoured or concocted evidence, composed of exaggeration, prejudice, and credulity, wellnigh incredible. Even Sir George Mackenzie, Lord Advocate of Scotland during the time of the greatest fury, admitted the indiscretion of ministerial zeal, and recommended that the wisest ministers should be chosen, and that those selected should proceed with caution. "I own," says the Rev. John Bell, Minister of the Gospel at Gladsmuir, in his MS., "Discourse of Witchcraft," 1705, "there has been much harm done to worthy and innocent persons in the common way of finding out witches, and in the means made use of for promoting the discovery of such wretches, and bringing them to justice ; that oftentimes old age, poverty, features, and ill fame, with such like grounds, not worthy

to be represented to a magistrate, have yet
moved many to suspect and defame their neighbours, to the unspeakable prejudice of Christian
charity; a late instance whereof we had in the
west, in the business of the sorceries exercised
upon the Laird of Bargarran's daughter, anno
1697, a time when persons of more goodness
and esteem than most of their calumniators were
defamed for witches, and which was occasioned
mostly by the forwardness and absurd credulity
of diverse otherwise worthy ministers of the
gospel, and some topping professors in and
about the city of Glasgow."

In the last forty years of the sixteenth century,
we have the astounding aggregate of no less
than eight thousand persons who suffered, almost
invariably by burning, for witchcraft. For about
the first decade, not more, perhaps, than forty
were so punished in a year, but towards the
close of the period alluded to, the annual death-
roll probably reached five hundred. The total
number of victims, strange to say, represented
even a larger proportion than those of the Holy
Office, during a corresponding space of time.
That during one period the Kirk should have
been more disposed to kindle the pile than was

the Inquisition, is, without doubt, a startling
fact.

For a time, at any rate, the population seemed
divided into only two great classes, witches and
witchfinders. The dark tales of witchcraft were
not even relieved by fairy folk-lore. There was,
perhaps, no little truth in what Cleland said in
his " Effigies Clericorum," when he attributed the
disappearance of Scottish fairies to the Reformation. In writing of Parnassus, he proceeds :—

> " There's als much virtue, sense, and pith,
> In Annan, or the Water of Nith,
> Which quietly slips by Dumfries,
> Als any water in all Greece.
> For there, and several other places,
> About mill-dams, and green brae faces,
> Both Elrich elfs and brownies stayed,
> And green-gown'd fairies daunc'd and played :
> When old John Knox, and other some,
> Began to plott the Haggs of Rome ;
> Then suddenly took to their heels,
> And did no more frequent these fields ;
> But if Rome's pipes perhaps they hear,
> Sure, for their interest they'll compear
> Again, and play their old hell's tricks."

As far as fairydom survived, however, it was
regarded as under the same guilt as witchcraft.

The harsh forbidding creed of the Kirk had
its influence in every direction ; and music,

instrumental at any rate, fell under its ban. During the sway of the Covenant, indeed, the Scottish minstrels were popularly supposed to be under the special care and protection of the devil. The Reverend Robert Kirk, author of the "Secret Commonwealth," attributed certain impressions produced by music to diabolical influence. "Irishmen," says he, "our northern Scottish, and our Athole men are so much addicted to, and delighted with harps and musick, as if, like King Saul, they were possessed with a forrein sport; only with this difference, that musick did put Saul's play-fellow asleep, but roused and awaked our men, vanquishing their own spirits at pleasure as if they were impotent of its powers, and unable to command it; for wee have seen some poor beggars of them chattering their teeth for cold, that how soon they saw the fire, and heard the harp, leap thorow the house like goats and satyrs." Without enlarging on the subject, may we not conclude that such an estimate of instrumental music as became common, especially in Covenanting days, had much to do with the prolonged antipathy of the Kirk to its introduction in worship?

But the Presbyterians went even further than this. At one time they declared that the bishops were cloven-footed and had no shadows, and that the curates themselves were, many of them, little better than wizards. The Episcopalians seem to have been regarded by the Presbyterians with little more favour than the Red Indians were by the early Puritan settlers in America. The extraordinary story of Salem witchcraft shows us that the Puritan clergy assured their people that the Red Indians were worshippers and agents of Satan ; and we can but faintly imagine the effect of this belief on the minds and tempers of those who were thinking of the Indians at every turn of daily life. The common people, always susceptible to exaggeration, had been preached into such a holy hatred of popery that they saw its type and shadow in everything which approached even to decency in worship ; so that, as a satirist expressed it, they thought it impossible they could ever lose their way to heaven, provided they left Rome behind them.

On the other hand, John Knox was deemed a skilful wizard by the Catholics in Scotland ; it was even said that in the churchyard of St. Andrews he raised Satan himself, wearing a

huge pair of horns on his head, at which blood-
curdling sight Knox's secretary became insane
and died. And in old Kirkton's "Secret and
True History," in his picturesque account of
the curious scene which was witnessed in Lithgow
upon the anniversary of the King's restoration,
we see that the Episcopal party lost no favour-
able opportunity of turning the tables on their
opponents. In the pageant they had an arch,
in the midst of which was a litany:

> "' From Covenants with uplifted hands,
>   From Remonstrators with associate bands,
>   From such Committees as govern'd this nation,
>   From Church Commissioners and their protestation,
>   Good Lord deliver us.'

"They hade also the picture of Rebellion in
religious habit, with the book Lex Rex in one
hand, and the causes of God's wrath in the other,
and this in midst of rocks, and reels, and kirk
stools, logs of wood, and spurs, and covenants,
acts of assembly, protestations, with this inscription, ' REBELLION IS THE MOTHER OF WITCH-
CRAFT.' "

But Episcopacy was abhorrent to the people
generally. A contemporary writer—a Presbyterian—candidly remarks, " I have known some

profane people that, if they committed an error over night, thought affronting a curate to-morrow a testimony of their repentance." This religious animosity had no doubt much to do with the belief that witchcraft was common among the Episcopalian clergy. The Reverend James Kirkton (before alluded to), a true son of the Kirk, writing at that time gravely relates, amongst several similar accusations, that one Gideen Penman said grace at the devil's table as his chaplain ; that one Thomson, the curate of Anstruther, was a "diabolic man," the wench who bore a lantern in front, as he returned from a visit, "affirming that she saw something like a black beast pass the bridge before him ; " and that the hated Archbishop Sharp, when assassinated, had "several strange things," and, in particular, "parings of nails," about his person. Archbishop Sharp was also charged with entertaining "the muckle black Deil" in his study at midnight, and of being "levitated" and dancing in the air ; and of Archbishop Adamson, men of learning like James, nephew and companion of Andrew Melville, believed that, as in the case of other witches, he had a familiar in the form of a hare, which once ran before him down the street.

It is a curious circumstance, as Pitcairn in his
"Criminal Trials" points out, that in almost all
the confessions of Scottish witches, their initia-
tion and many of their gatherings were said to
have taken place within churches, or at least the
surrounding ground, and a certain derisive form
of service was carried out. James VI. of Scotland and I. of England was, in the matter
of witches, undoubtedly the greatest royal expert that ever lived.   His famous dialogue,
" Dæmonologie," in which he carefully classifies
witches, describes their ceremonials, and details
their various characteristics, did much to en-
courage popular credulity and the spirit of
persecution. "Witches," he affirms, "ought to
be put to death, according to the laws of God,
the civil and imperial law, and the municipal
law of all Christian nations; yea, to spare the
life, and not strike whom God bids strike, and so
severely punish so odious a treason against God,
is not only unlawful, but, doubtless, as great a
sin as was Saul's sparing Agag."   He even con-
tended that, because the crime was generally
abominable, evidence in proof might be received
which would be rejected in other offences, and
that the only means of escape to be offered was

through the ordeal. If we only remember that
Luther said he would burn every one of them,
urging that there must be witches because the
Bible says, "Thou shalt not suffer a witch to
live," we shall wonder less at the credulity of
the witch-hunting king.

The principal witch cases and trials in Scotland may be said to date from the conspiracy
of devils to prevent James's union with the
Princess Anne of Denmark. "An overwhelm-
ing tempest at sea during the voyage of these
anti-papal, anti-diabolic, royal personages was
the appointed means of their destruction." To
describe the trial of those who were implicated
as the human agents, even though it may be
one of the most extraordinary and weirdly fascinating stories in the annals of Scottish witchcraft, would be beyond the scope of this
article; it is fully related in an exceedingly
scarce black-letter pamphlet—"Newes from
Scotland, declaring the damnable Life of Doctor
Fian, a notable Sorcerer, who was burned at
Edenbrough in Januarie last, 1591; which
Doctor was Register to the Devill, that sundry
times preached at North-Baricke Kirke to a
number of notorious Witches, &c." It may be

noted, however, that "Agnis Sampson, which was the elder witch," at last confessed, "before the king's majestie and his councell," "that upon the night of Allhollon-Even, shee was accompanied, as well with the persons aforesaide, as also with a great many other witches, to the number of two hundreth, and that all they together went to sea, each one in a riddle, or cive, and went in the same very substantially, with flaggons of wine, making merrie and drinking by the way in the same riddles, or cives, to the kirke of North-Barrick, in Lowthian, and that after they had landed, tooke handes on the lande, and daunced this reill, or short daunce, singing all with one voice :—

Commer, goe ye before, commer, goe ye ;
Gif ye will not goe before, commer, let me !'

At which time shee confessed, that this Geillis Duncane (another of those charged) did goe before them, playing this reill or daunce uppon a small trumpe, called a Jewe's trumpe, untill they entered into the Kerk of North-Barrick.

"These confessions made the king in a wonderful admiration, and sent for the saide Geillis Duncane, who, upon the like trumpe, did play the saide daunce before the kinges majestie, who, in respect of the strangeness of these matters, tooke great delight to be present at their examinations. Item, the said Agnis Sampson confessed that the divell being then at North Barrick Kirke, attending their comming, in the habit or likenesse of a man, and seeing that they tarried over long, hee at their comming enjoyned them all to a penance. . . . . and having made his ungodly exhortations, wherein he did greatly inveigh against the King of Scotland, he received their oathes for their good and true service towards him, and departed; which done, they returned to sea and so home again.

"At which time the witches demanded of the divell, why he did beare such hatred to the king? who answered, by reason the king is the greatest enemie hee hath in the world."

Spottiswoode also tells a fantastic story in connection with this Agnes Sampson, Dr John Fian, Geillie Duncan, and others, meeting the devil at North Berwick kirk, of black candles round about the pulpit, of the devil calling the roll and preaching a sermon, and of the rifling of three graves for magical cookery. Of Francis, Earl of Bothwell, who was accused of being associated with Dr Fian in his magical conspiracy against the king, and who was also imprisoned for having conspired the king's death by sorcery, we have this note attached to a curious discourse, from Mr Robert Bruce's Sermons, preached at Edinburgh, November 9th, 1589—"At the which time the Earle Bothwell made his publicke repentance in the church." It will not be forgotten that, in "Tam o' Shanter," Burns depicts a witches' meeting in Alloway Kirk :—

> "A winnock-bunker in the east,
> There sat auld Nick, in shape o' beast;
> A towzie tyke, black, grim, and large,
> To gie them music was his charge :
> He screw'd the pipes and gart them skirl,
> Till roof and rafters a' did dirl.—
> Coffins stood round like open presses,
> That show'd the dead in their last dresses;
> And by some devilish cantraip sleight
> Each in its cauld hand held a light."

As typical of the evidence afforded by parochial inquisitions, and on which death sentences were based, the following may be taken :—

"Isabel Roby.—She is indicted to have bidden her gudeman, when he went to St. Fergus to buy cattle, that if he bought any before his home-coming, he should go three times 'woodersonis' about them, and then take three 'ruggis' off a

dry hillock, and fetch home to her. Also, that
dwelling at Ardmair, there came in a poor man
craving alms, to whom she offered milk, but he
refused it, because, as he then presently said,
she had three folks' milk and her own in the
pan ; and when Elspet Mackay, then present,
wondered at it, he said, 'Marvel not, for she
has thy farrow kye's milk also in her pan.'
Also, she is commonly seen in the form of a
hare, passing through the town, for as soon as
the hare vanishes out of sight, she appears."

"Margaret Rianch, in Green Cottis, was seen
in the dawn of the day by James Stevens embrac-
ing every nook of John Donaldson's house three
times, who continually thereafter was diseased,
and at last died. She said to John Ritchie, when
he took a tack (a piece of ground) in the Green
Cottis, that his gear from that day forth should
continually decay, and so it came to pass. Also,
she cast a number of stones in a tub, amongst
water, which thereafter was seen dancing. When
she clips her sheep, she turns the bowl of the
shears three times in her mouth. Also, James
Stevens saw her meeting John Donaldson's
'hoggs' (sheep a year old) in the burn of the
Green Cottis, and casting the water out between

her feet backward, in the sheep's face, and so they all died."

These charges were considered sufficient by the Presbytery of Kincardine, and were duly signed by " Mr Jhone Ros, Minister at Lumphanan."

The following, under date February 8th, 1719, will, however, more clearly illustrate the manner in which an accused person was examined by Kirk authority :—

" The said day, Mr William Innes, minister of Thurso, having interrogat Margaret Nin-Gilbert, who was apprehended Fryday last, on suspicion of witchcraft, as follows :—1*mo*, Being interrogat, If ever there was any compact between her and the devil ? Confessed, That as she was travelling some time bygone, in ane evening, the devill met with her in the way in the likeness of a man, and engaged her to take on with him, which she consented to ; and that she said she knew him to be the devil or he parted with her. 2*do*, Being interrogat, If ever the devil appeared afterwards to her ? Confessed, That sometimes he appeared in the likeness of a great black horse, and other times riding on a black horse, and that he appeared sometimes in the likeness of a black cloud, and sometimes like a black henn. 3*to*, Being interrogat, If she was in the house of William Montgomerie, mason in the Burnside of Scrabster, especially on that night when that house was dreadfully infested with severall catts, to that degree that W. M. foresaid was obliged to use sword, durk, and ax in beating and fraying away these catts? Confessed, That she was bodily present yr, and that the said M. had broke her legg either by the durk or ax, which legg since has fallen off from the other part of her body; and that she was in the likeness of a feltered cat, night forsaid, in the said house; and that Margaret Olsone was there in the likeness of a catt also, who, being stronger than she, did cast her on Montgomerie's durk when her legg was broken. 4*to*, Being interrogat, How she could be bodily present and yet invisible? Declares, She might have been seene, but could give no account by what means her body was rendered invisible. She declares, that severall other women were present there that night in the other end of the house. Being interrogat, How they came not to be seene, seeing they were not there in the likeness of catts, as were others condescended on? Declares, The devil

did hide and conceall them by raising a dark
mist or fog to skreen them from being seen. . . .
6*to*, Being interrogat, What brought her and her
accomplices to Montgomerie's house? Answered,
They were doing no harm there. To which Mr
Innes replyed, that the disturbing and infesting
a man's house with hideous noises, and cryes of
catts, was a great wrong done to him, having a
natural tendency to fright the family and children.
The premisses are attested to be the ingenuous
confession of Margaret Nin-Gilbert, *alias* Gilbert-
son, by William Innes, minister of Thurso. . . .
Nota, That upon a vulgar report of witches
having the devil's marks in their bodies, Margaret
Olsone being tryed in the shoulders, where there
were severall small spots, some read, some blewish,
after a needle was driven in with great force
almost to the eye, she felt it not. Mr Innes and
Mr Oswald, ministers, were witnesses to this."
In another case it is recorded that "Mr John
Aird, minister, put a prin in the accused's
shoulder (where she carries the devill's mark) up
to the heid, and no bluid followed theiron, nor
she shrinking thereat."

The foregoing "dittay," conjointly with the
confessions of so many of the accused, inevitably

prompts the anxious question—how could it be
that these persons declared themselves guilty of
an impossible offence when the admission must
have sealed their doom? The assumption that
the victim preferred being killed at once to living
on, subject to suspicion, insult, and ill-will, under
the imputation of having dealt with the devil, cannot here, any more than in the astounding cases
recorded in connection with Salem witchcraft,
cover anything like the whole ground. There
can be little doubt now that the sufferers under
nervous disturbances, the subjects of abnormal
conditions, found themselves in possession of
strange faculties, and thought themselves able to
do new and wonderful things. When urged to
explain how it was, they perhaps could only
suppose that it was by some " evil spirit," and
except where there was an intervening agency to
be named, the only supposition was that the
intercourse between the Evil Spirit and themselves was direct. It is impossible, as an Edinburgh Reviewer has remarked, even now to
witness the curious phenomena of somnambulism
and catalepsy without a keen sense of how
natural and even inevitable it was for similar
subjects of the middle ages and in Puritan

times to believe themselves ensnared by Satan,
and actually endowed with his gifts, and to
confess their calamity, as the only relief to their
scared and miserable minds.   It would also
seem as though some of these unfortunate women
credited themselves with certain powers because
others so credited them, and believed that they
could perform deeds of witchcraft because their
neighbours declared they could.

But let us turn again to the Kirk Session
Records, than which we can find no better
sources of information.   During the years 1649-
1650, for instance, the witch fires seemed never
to have ceased burning.   In the Lowlands one,
John Kincaid, and another, George Cathie, were
expert searchers.   In 1650 the Presbytery of
Biggar called on the Presbytery of Haddington,
as well as the civil power, to secure Cathie's
services whenever they were required.   In 1649
John Kincaid received from the minister and
elders of Stowe for the "broding of Margret
Durham, 6lb."   His colleage Cathie once condemned as witches twelve people in Crauford-
Douglas on the evidence of a lunatic.

And here are a few significant extracts from the
Tyninghame Kirk Session Records :—" January

11, 1629.—This day James Fairlie preichit, the minister being at Edinr., at comand of the presbiterie, to assist Mr Js. Home, minister at Dunbar, anent the tryall of ane woman suspect of witchcraft in the parish of Dunbar—viz., Issbell Yong, in Eist Barns." She was accused of both inflicting and curing diseases, and was burnt for witchcraft. "17 September 1649.—Janet Nicolson execut and brunt at Hails for witchcraft. 25 November.—Item: According to the ordinance, he intimate out of the pulpit if any had any delations against Agnes Raleigh, in East Barns, suspect of witchcraft, and apprehendit there for that, they come to the session of Dunbar upon Tysday, or the presbyterie on Thursday next. On Monday the witches at Wittinghame brunt, being three in number. 9 December.—Intimation maid from the pulpit anent Patrick Yorston and Christian Yorston, in Wittinghame, if any in this parish either knew or have any delations against both or either of them, that they show it to the kirk-session. 6 January 1650.—Some of our pepell confronted with some witches in Prestonkirk parish. 13 January.—The minister demandit the elders if they knew of any suspect of witchcraft, and shew them that they were to search diligentlie such as are delated be the witches at Prestonkirk parish, when the searchers cam. Upon Tysday ane man in Wittinghame brunt for witchcraft. Upon Wednesday, the 23 of January, six people at Staintoune parish brunt. 3 February.—Item: Reported that the searchers of the witches were not yet returned from the southe, and in the meantime that Agnes Kirkland and David Stewart shall be apprehendit. On Thursday Agnes Kirkland and David Stewart, bothe of this parish, were imprisoned. Wednesday.—I (the minister) went to Dunbar, being ordained thairto, whair ten witches were execut.

"10 February.—This day the session sett doon orders aboot the watching of those that are apprehendit for witchcraft nichtlie, appointing ane roll of all the parishe to be taken up and six to watch everie nicht, and twa everie day thair, tyme aboot in order, qlk accordinglie was done. Upon the 20 of February the searcher in Tranent cam and found the mark on those that were suspect of witchcraft, and shortlie thairafter they confessit. 3 Mairch.— Item: Ordains the watch to be keipit preceisely, and ane elder to watch everie nicht in turn with

them, qlk they did, and promeisit to continue.
The minister shew his diligence in going to
those suspect of witchcraft, both in the day and
nicht-time, in examining of them, and in praying for them, both privatelie and publiklie, and
performing all the other duties recognisit or
practised in such cases, qlk the session heartilie
and unanimouslie acknowledge and approved.
Upon Tysday, the 1st Mairch, the pepell given
up be Agnes Kirkland and David Stewart, both
in this parish and Prestonkirk parish, confronted
with them, and did pass from some and stand
by others.   29 Mairch.—Appoints the watch
to be better keipit, qlk they promeisit to do.
31 Mairch.—Item : Because the commission
anent the witches was not as yet come, it was
thocht gude to have ane cair of them still.   The
elders shew it was hard to get pepell to watch
all the day, albeit the watch was preceisly keipit
all the nicht ; and thairfor it behoved them to
tak something out of the box, or rather to
borrow it, to give to some wha had watched
this eight days byegane—viz., Robert Nisbet
and George Ker, given to them 3lbs., and efter
the burning of the witches.   7 April.—Item :
The minister shew to the elders anent David

Stewart and Agnes Kirkland, that now the commission to put them to assize had come eist to our hands, and that some that were appointed and put in the same did meet heir on Setterday, and appointed all things to be done, and in what manner; and Tysday next to be the day wherin to put them to an assize; and thairfor to appoint the watch to be well observed this twa nichts to come, and all the elders and honest men to be present on Tysday, wherunto they consentit. 9, Tysday, 1650.—David Stewart and Agnes Kirkland were execut. 14 April.—George Shorthous intromits with what belongs to Agnes Kirkland; promeisit to the session 12lbs. out of Agnes Kirkland's readiest gudes and gear, and find the box lykwys, if by any means he culd." There is no necessity to add anything to the ghastly simplicity of such sentences as these.

The expenses incurred in these matters by the Kirk cannot be considered trifling. There are significant entries like the following: "21 July 1661.—Given for candle to watch the witch, 11s.;" but much fuller statements are also given. In 1633 two poor victims, "William Coke and Alison Dick, witches," were burned, as the Kirk

Session Records testify, on the sands at Kirk-caldy. And in connection with that event these were the "Extraordinary Disbursements":—

In primus—To Mr John Millar when he went to Prestoun for a man to try them,	£2	7	0
To the man of Culross when he went away the first time, . .	0	12	0
Item—For cales for the witches, . . .	1	4	0
Item—For purchasing the commission, . .	0	3	0
Item—For one to go to Finmouth for the Laird to sit upon their assize as judge, ...	0	6	0
Item—For harden to be jumps to them, .	3	10	0
Item—For making of them, ...	0	6	0
Summa, Kirk's part,	£17	10	0

In primus—For 10 loads of coal to burn them,	£3	6	8
Item—For a tar barrel, ...	0	14	0
Item—For towes, ...	0	6	0
Item—To him that brought the executioner, .	2	18	0
Item—To the executioner for his pains, .	8	14	0
Item—For his expenses here, . . .	0	16	4
Item—For one to go to Finmouth for the Laird, . .	0	6	0
Summa, Toun's part,	£17	1	0

The other items, the cost of which would bring the "Summa, Kirk's part," to £17, 10s., are not supplied.

The severity with which the witches were

sometimes treated during imprisonment is sufficiently indicated by the following entries, 1597 :—

Item. To Alexander Reid, smyth, for twa pair
of scheckellis to the Witches in the
Stepill, ...   xxxii*sh*

Item. To John Justice, for burning upon the
cheik of four seurerall personis suspect
of witchcraft and baneschit,   .   .   xxvi*sh*. viii*d*.

Item. Givin to Alexander Home, for macking
of joggis, stapillis, and lockis to the
witches, during the haill tyme forsaid,   xlvi*sh*. viii*d*.
Expense on witches,   aucht-score, xlii*li*, xvii*sh*. iiii*d*.

It could not be supposed that ministers,
who were so zealous in attacking witchcraft,
would be permitted by the supernatural powers
to go scot-free.   In the evidence given in the
Mohra witch commission, held in Sweden in
1670, the minister of the district testified that
having been suffering from a painful headache,
he could account for the unusual severity of the
attack only by supposing that the witches had
celebrated one of their infernal dances upon his
head while asleep in bed ; and one of them, in
accordance with this conjecture, acknowledged
that the devil had sent her with a sledge-
hammer to drive a nail into the temples of the
obnoxious clergyman, but the hardness of his

skull mercifully saved him. And in Scotland the Renfrewshire witches were charged with roasting the effigy of a Rev. Mr Hardy, after having dipped it into a decoction composed of ale and water; while, in 1622, one of the accusations against Margaret Wallace, burnt for witchcraft, was " that being conveined before the Kirk Session of Glasco 5 or 6 years since, by Mr Archibald Glen, minister at Carmunnock, for killing Robert Muir, his good brother, by witchcraft; she, to be revenged, laid on him ane uncouth sickness, whereof the said Mr Archibald, sweating, died; to which it was answered, that in truth the said Mr Archibald died of a consumption of his lights." In a curious sheet, " Endorism, or a strange Relation of Dreamers or Spirits that trouble the Minister's House of Kinross," we read how a minister was molested in 1718. For some time " they could eat no meat but what was full of pins "; "a stone thrown down the chimney wambled a space in the floor, and then took a flight out at the window. Also there was thrown in the fire the minister's Bible, which would not burn; but a plate and two silver spoons thrown in, melted immediately; also what bread is fired, were the meal never so fine, it's all made useless ; and many other things, which are both needless and sinful to mention. Now, is it not very sad that such a good and godly family should be so molested, that employ their time no other way but by praying, reading, and serious meditation, while others, who are wicked livers all their lifetime, and avowedly serve that wicked one, are never troubled."

And let it not be inferred that Kirk Sessions were, without exception, quick to condemn. We find in the records of the Kirk Session at East-wood that a woman, who was delated for using charms at Hallow-even and who confessed, was sentenced to be rebuked before the congregation ; and in the records of Lanark Presbytery (1630), that another woman, charged with consulting with charmers and " burying a child's clothes betwixt three lairds' lands for health," was saved by penitence from punishment. And sometimes the consideration of cases, far more serious than these in the eyes of the grave Kirk Session, was wisely postponed, and postponed for ever, for we hear no more of the matter.

But in 1735 the reaction, which had long made itself felt, found something like adequate expression in the repeal of the statutes against witchcraft, and, notwithstanding the action of such as the Seceders from the Established Church of Scotland, who inveighed against this repeal as iniquitous, prosecutions for witchcraft entirely ceased. These "Seceders," who claimed to be the real representatives of the Church's teaching, were so offended that, in the annual Confession of National and Personal Sins, printed in an act of their Associate Presbytery at Edinburgh, 1743, the Penal Statutes against witches are specially mentioned as having been repealed by Parliament, contrary to the express Law of God!

And with this reference the consideration of witchcraft and the Kirk may conveniently and appropriately end.

Birth and Baptisms, Customs and Superstitions.

SOME strange customs, the origin of which does not appear to have been traced, but which probably came down from the dark ages of Celtic paganism, were performed in bygone times on the birth of a child. When such an important event in family history was expected, a rich cheese was made, which, when the anticipation was realised, was divided among the women who, on such occasions, were injudiciously allowed to crowd the chamber. A lighted slip of fir-wood was whirled three times round the bed, with the superstitious idea of averting evil influences. The new-born babe was next dipped into a vessel of cold water, tempered in a very slight degree by dropping a burning coal into it. This may have been done with the Spartan idea of rendering the child hardy. If a boy, it was afterwards wrapped in a woman's chemise; if a girl, in a man's shirt. The idea underlying this custom is not clear. Women were not allowed

194

to touch the child without first crossing themselves. The tiny creature was not to be referred to in terms of admiration, lest it should be "forespoken," which implied consequences prejudicial to its future welfare.

After the mother's recovery, friends and neighbours assembled to congratulate the parents, and drink to the child's future prosperity. This gathering was known as the *cummer-fealls*, or the gossips' wake, concerning which custom the Kirk Session of Dunfermline made, in 1645, one of the most sensible enactments to be found on the minutes of those bodies. Considering, it is recorded, "the inconveniences arising therefrom, as mainly the loss and abusing of so much time, which may be better employed in attending to business at home, by such as frequent the occasions thereof, and the prejudice which persons lying in child-bed receive, both in health and means, being forced, not only to bear company to such as come to visit, but also to provide for their coming more than is either necessary or their estate may bear," the Session inhibited "all visits of this kind, and for the end foresaid, under the pain of being, for the first fault, censured by the Session, and there to be obliged to acknowledge their fault, and, for the next, to make public confession of their fault before the whole congregation."

Other singular practices were observed in connection with the baptism of a child. It was placed in a basket, on which a white cloth was spread, with some bread and cheese, and the basket was suspended by a crook over the fire-place, and swung round three times. This was said to be done to counteract the evil influence of fairies and other malignant spirits. The bread and cheese were offered to the first person met on the way to the church, and rejection of it was thought to presage future evil to the babe. When several children were baptised at the same time, the boys were presented for the rite first, for it was thought that, if a girl obtained priority, she would in after time be disfigured by a beard.

Baptism was at one time refused to the children of persons outside the communion of the Reformed Church. In 1567, the Countess of Argyle was ordered by the Assembly to "make public repentance in the chapel royal of Stirling, one Sunday, in time of preaching," for assisting at the baptism of the royal infant, afterwards

James VI., "in a papistical manner."   And even in 1716, registration of baptism was refused to the child of Harry Foulis, son of Sir James Foulis, on the ground that it had been baptised by a minister of the Episcopal Church.   Thereupon the father procured the baptismal register from the session clerk, and made the entry himself, appending a statement of the circumstances.

The sacrament of baptism has been the subject of much controversy in the Scottish church, especially in the seventeenth century, when everyone born north of the Tweed seems to have been, more or less, a theological disputant.   In the First Book of Discipline, in the framing of which Knox had much to do, it was laid down that, "In baptism, we acknowledge nothing to be used except the element of water only ; wherefore, whosoever presumeth to use oil, salt, wax, spittle, conjuration, and crossing, accuseth the perfect institution of Jesus Christ of imperfection, for it was void of all such inventions devised by men."   The abjuring of conjuration seems to refer to a formula of exorcism prescribed by the first Prayer Book of Edward VI., to be used in the rite of baptism.

Concerning the use of the cross in baptism

there has been an enormous amount of controversy, and very opposite views are still held.
Dr Renaud, who wrote a ponderous volume on
the subject in 1607, says: "It is as unfit to
make a cross a memorial of Christ as for a child
to make much of the halter or gallows wherewith
his father was hanged." The Service Book of
1637 enjoined the use of the cross in baptism,
and as that book is said, by Spalding, to have
been introduced in many parts of the country, it
may be concluded that the practice existed thereafter in some Scotch churches. As to other
baptismal ceremonies, Dr Edgar observes, in
his "Old Church Life in Scotland," that the
principles laid down by Knox "are the principles
on which the Church of Scotland has always
acted. She has uniformly endeavoured, except
during a brief interlude of Anglican innovation
prior to 1638, to make her sacramental forms
square with the pattern and precepts set before
her in Scripture."

Another question concerning which there has
been much controversy, is the lawfulness or
otherwise of private baptism. In 1618, when
the historically famous "five articles," framed by
James I., as king of both England and Scotland,

were sent to the General Assembly for sanction and approval, their adoption by that body raised a storm of indignation and opposition which was not allayed until they were abjured by the General Assembly in 1638, and the proceedings of the Assembly held at Perth in 1618 were declared null and void.

One of the articles objected to was that which pronounced "that baptism might be administered at home when the infant could not conveniently be brought to church." This was objected to as papistical, and denounced as introducing a new and false doctrine of baptism, calculated to create a superstitious belief that there was some spiritual efficacy in the act of sprinkling a few drops of water on an infant's face, in the name of the Trinity, thereby giving ground for the belief that baptism is essential to salvation. This doctrine, though taught by the Church of England, has not been accepted by the Church of Scotland since the Reformation.

Moreover, as non-attendance at the services of the Church was regarded as contrary to good order, it was objected that the administration of baptism in private houses would allow Christian privileges to be enjoyed without compliance with

Christian duty. If a child was to be accepted and declared a member of the Church, the act should be performed by the whole congregation, and not by the minister alone. For at least a hundred years this was strongly and firmly insisted upon. Some doubt seems to have been felt in 1643, as to whether the Westminster Assembly would adopt the Scottish view of the question, as baptisms were very commonly performed in private houses by ministers of the English Presbyterian Church. It was with much satisfaction, therefore, that the news was received in Scotland that the Assembly had affirmed the necessity of public baptism.

The Directory for Public Worship in the Presbyterian Church states, accordingly, that baptism "is not to be administered in private places, or privately, but in the place of public worship, and in the face of the congregation, where the people may most conveniently see and hear; and not in the places where fonts, in the time of Popery, were unfitly and superstitiously placed," that is, near the church door, and behind the backs of the congregation. The view held by Presbyterians since the Reformation thus became the law of the Church; and the General

Assembly, in 1690, strictly enjoined that baptism should not be administered elsewhere than in church, and before the coi ,regation. But in this matter, as in some others, there appears to have been a laxity in enforcing the rule of the church, which has gone on increasing. Wodrow stated, in 1718, that private baptisms were unknown in the Church of Scotland, except in Edinburgh and Glasgow; and only two years later the Synod of Glasgow and Ayr had to repeat the injunction of 1690. What the state of things in this respect is at the present day we are told by Dr Edgar, who, as minister of Mauchline, must be considered to speak from experience. He says that, "in some parishes there are ten private baptisms for every one public baptism; and these private baptisms are never challenged as irregular, unlawful, or deserving of censure."

Registers of baptisms have been kept, with more or less regularity, from the time of the Reformation; and these show that, in some parishes at least, private baptisms had become very frequent about the middle of the eighteenth century. In referring to the evidence of the parish register of Mauchline on this matter, the writer just quoted says: "Although such baptisms were a violation of Church order, I cannot help remarking that Church order was not, in this instance, clearly founded on the evangelical principle professed by our forefathers, that all procedure in Church ritual should be conform to the precept or example of Scripture. It seems quite certain that, in the days of the Apostles, baptism was not always, if ever, administered in the place of public worship and in the face of the congregation. The eunuch of Ethiopia, Cornelius the centurion, St. Paul himself, and the gaoler at Philippi were each baptised privately."

The Church of Scotland has been more strict in upholding the rule of the Westminster Directory, that baptism "is not to be administered, in any case, by any private person." This also, it may be remarked, is not in strict accordance with the principle of the Christian Church in its early ages, as set forth by some of the Fathers; and down even to the present day the Church of England, while discountenancing lay baptism as a rule, has recognised its validity in cases of necessity. The recorded instances of refusal to admit evidence of lay baptism in the Church of Scotland are, however, chiefly cases in which the rite had been performed by deposed ministers. In 1708, a Kilmarnock man was cited to appear before the Kirk Session for having had a child irregularly baptised by a deposed minister, namely, Macmillan, the founder of the Reformed Presbyterian Church. No further proceedings appear, however, to have been taken. Similar cases occurred in 1715 and 1721, the General Assembly in the former case, and the Presbytery of Ayr in the latter, merely pronouncing the baptisms null and void.

Some differences have to be noted between the Churches of Scotland and England with regard to the forms and customs connected with baptisms. The former is the more strict with regard to the sponsors of the children to be baptised. The Westminster Directory states that the child is to be presented at the font by its father, or in the case of his unavoidable absence, by some Christian friend in his place; and in 1712 the General Assembly enacted that no other sponsor than a parent should be received at a baptism, "unless the parents be dead, or absent, or grossly ignorant, or under scandal, or contumacious to discipline; in which cases, some fit person (and if it can be, one related to the child,) should be sponsor."

Not only was the Church more strict in this matter in Scotland than in England, but the nature of the sponsion was different. In Knox's Liturgy, the sponsors are not regarded as proxies for the child, but are required to make a declaration of their own faith, in which they engage to instruct the child. As the matter is well put by Dr Hill, "the parents do not make any promise for the child, but they promise for themselves that nothing shall be wanting, on their part, to engage the child to undertake, at some future time, that obligation which he cannot then understand."

In the latter half of the seventeenth and the first of the eighteenth century, the Kirk Sessions had as much to do in repressing undue gatherings at the font as on the occasion of wedding festivities. In 1622 the Kirk Session of Aberdeen, considering "that it is come in custom that every base servile man in the town, when he has a bairn to be baptised, invites twelve or sixteen persons to be his gossips and god-fathers to his bairn," whereas the old custom was not to invite more than two, ordered that in future only two or at most four persons should be allowed to appear in that capacity. In 1681 an Act of Parliament prohibited the attendance at baptisms of more than four witnesses, in addition to parents and children, brothers and sisters; and in 1720 the Kirk Session of Kilmarnock made an ordinance that "only so many women as are necessary attend infants that are carried to the church to be baptised, and the Session think three sufficient."

Down to the time of the Westminster Assembly, it seems to have been the custom in Scotland for parents, at the baptism of a child, to repeat the Creed. But in the Westminster Directory the father is merely required to promise that he will bring up the child "in the nurture and admonition of the Lord." Nevertheless, many Kirk Sessions overlaid this requirement with regulations of their own devising. In 1615, the Kirk Session of Lasswade ordained that "no children of ignorant persons be baptised, except the father first lay one poynd of ten shillings, and a month shall be granted to learn the Lord's Prayer, Belief, and Ten Commandments, with some competent knowledge of the sacraments and catechism, which he performing, his poynd shall be returned, otherwise forfeited." In 1700 an application to the Kirk Session of Galston for the baptism of a child was refused, on the ground that the father "did not attend diets of catechising." On his promising to attend in future, and submitting to rebuke for his previous non-attendance, the child was allowed to be baptised. More than three-quarters of a century later, that is, in 1779, a man who had applied to the Kirk Session of Mauchline for the baptism of a child was subjected to a theological examination much too stiff for him ; but on promising to study the knotty points propounded to him, and signing an undertaking to that effect in the minute-book, he was allowed to present the child for baptism, though the permission seems to have been regarded as a great favour.

As in England, so also in Scotland, the registration of baptisms was required at a period long antecedent to the statutary obligation to register births. Old sessional records show that fees were paid, but it is a disputed question whether these were for baptism or for registration.   Dunlop, in his "Parochial Law," quotes a legal opinion to the effect that "as to baptisms, what is paid on that account is for obtaining the Kirk Session's order for baptism, and recording that order." But an entry in the records of the Kirk Session of Galston, in 1640, after prescribing the fee to be paid for baptism, adds—"and there shall be no more exacted of any that come to this kirk for all time coming, except they desire the baptism registered, and in that case to satisfy the reader therefore, which is hereby declared to be other four shillings Scottish."

There are several curious entries in Kirk Sessional Records, showing that those parochial bodies were as zealous in restricting the customary festivities at christening parties as they have, in another paper, been shown to have been in repressing undue feasting at weddings. With respect of the former, the interference of Kirk Sessions was preceded by that of the Scottish Parliament, by which assembly it was enacted, in 1581, "that no banquets shall be at any upsitting after baptising of bairns in time coming, under the pain of twenty pounds, to be paid by every person doing the contrary." In

1621 it was further enacted that, "no person use any manner of dessert of wet and dry confections at marriage banqueting, baptism feasting, or any meals, except the fruits growing in Scotland, as also figs, raisins, plum dames, almonds and other unconfected fruits, under the pain of a thousand marks *toties quoties.*"

These enactments appear, however, to have had little effect. In 1695 the Kirk Session of Greenock ordained that "persons having their children baptised on the Sabbath day abstain from keeping banquets and convening people at such occasions on that day, whereby much idle discourse and sin may be evited." In 1701 it was very seriously complained by the Kirk Session of Kilmarnock that feasts continued to be held on Sundays after baptisms, and it was ordered that children should be baptised on the weekly sermon day (Thursday), except in case of necessity. But, either through attachment to old customs, or want of inclination to attend the week-day sermon, children continued to be presented for baptism on Sunday, and in 1720 the Session again ordered "that none make or hold feasts at baptising their children on the Lord's day."

In conformity with the Registration Act for

Scotland, passed in 1854, all parish registers are deposited in the Registry Office then established in Edinburgh. Most of the registers of births commence about the middle of the seventeenth century, those of only fifteen parishes, out of about nine hundred, dating from the preceding century. The register of baptisms of Errol, Perthshire, commences in 1553, but the entries for the years preceding 1573 are transcribed from an older register which has been lost. Many of the older registers have been injured by damp, others by fire, and not a few have suffered from the negligence of their custodians. In many of them blanks occur. In some instances session clerks of the sixteenth century recorded in their registers events unconnected with their own parishes. The clerk of the Kirk Session of Aberdeen made an entry in the register of the birth of James VI., who was born at Edinburgh, loyally and piously adding, in the curious spelling of the period (which in previous extracts in this paper, has been modernised,) "quhame God preserve in guid helth and in the feir of God, to do justice in punishing of wrayng and in manttinyen the trewht all the dais of his lyfe. So be itt."

Marriage Laws and Customs.

THE laws relating to marriage differ so much in Scotland from those under which dwellers south of the Tweed live, that no comparison of social and religious life in the two countries can be made without knowledge of them. In no part of Christendom have the ecclesiastical laws relating to the relations of the sexes been more strict, or more strictly enforced, than in Scotland, and in no other have there been more irregularities. It was not until more than twenty years after the Reformation that the custom of "handfasting," which had come down from old Celtic times, fell into disrepute and consequent disuse. By this term was understood cohabitation for a year, the couple being then free to separate, unless they agreed to make the union permanent. Lindsay, the chronicler, says of Alexander Dunbar, son of the sixth Earl of Moray, and Isobel Innes, —"This Isobel was but handfast with him, and deceased before the marriage." When

Margaret, widow of James IV., sued for a divorce from the Earl of Angus, she pleaded that he had been handfasted to Jane Douglas, "and by reason of that pre-contract could not be her lawful husband." How such marriages were regarded at that time is shown by the fact that the marriage was dissolved by the Pope, though the issue of the Queen's marriage with Angus was pronounced legitimate.

Sir John Sinclair's "Statistical Account of Scotland" contains a report from the minister of Eskdale Muir, referring to the practice of handfasting as existing in that parish, under ecclesiastical sanction, at a period anterior to the Reformation. At a fair held there, unmarried men chose women to be handfasted with them, and a monk from Melrose Abbey visited the place annually, to marry those couples who wished the union to be made permanent. The first check given to the practice appears to have been the decree of the Kirk Session of Aberdeen, in 1562, that persons cohabiting under the sanction of a handfast contract of marriage should be united in lawful wedlock. But though this practice was discontinued, and those who wished to be thought respectable obtained the blessing of the Church on their marriage, irregularities continued to exist, and even to be permitted. An acknowledgment by a couple that they were husband and wife, either orally or in writing, followed or preceded by cohabitation, was regarded as a valid marriage, both by the Church and by society. In 1563, however, the General Assembly of the Church ruled that no contract of marriage so made should be recognised until the parties had submitted themselves to the discipline of the Church, and the contract had been verified by witnesses of good repute.

The custom of betrothal was very general, but it varied in form in different parts of the kingdom. The presentation of an "engagement ring," as in England, is not found among these forms, nor does it appear that the sanction of parents was thought necessary ; but after the contract was made it was usual for them to be informed and their sanction sought. Among the upper and middle classes there was usually a betrothal feast, but among the classes living by manual labour this was dispensed with. Dr Rogers says, in his " Social Life in Scotland," that—" In betrothal, the parties usually moistened with the tongue the thumbs of their right hands, and then pressed them together. The violation of a contract so consecrated was considered tantamount to an act of perjury." Another form of betrothal was the clasping of. hands across a stream. In this way Burns, the laureate of the Scottish peasantry, and Mary Campbell vowed fidelity. In some counties silver coins were exchanged by plighted lovers, or a worn one was broken between them, each retaining one of the halves.

Marriages regarded by the ecclesiastical courts and Kirk Sessions as "regular" have always, from a long period anterior to the Reformation, been preceded by the publication of banns. In 1569 a case came before the General Assembly which shows the successive steps taken at that time before the solemnisation of a marriage. It is recorded that "ane promise of marriage made, before the readers and elders, in ane reformit church, the parties contractit compeirs before the minister and session, and requires their banns to be proclaimit." In 1575 the question came before the General Assembly, whether the form of mutual declaration prior to the publication of banns should be longer continued; and it was

ruled that it should be considered sufficient for
the names of the parties desiring proclamation
of banns to be given to the session clerk.
Banns were ordered to be published, as in
England, on three successive Sundays; but,
after the Reformation, it was ruled that, on
payment of a larger fee, one public announce-
ment should be held sufficient, the words "for
the first, second, and third time" being used.

It became customary towards the close of the
sixteenth century for security to be given, with
the notice of banns, for the solemnisation of the
marriage, two friends of the parties depositing
with the clerk a sum of money as a guarantee,
and that for more than one purpose. In 1570
the Assembly ordered that "promise of marriage
shall be made according to the order of the
reformed Kirk to the minister, exhorter, or
reader, taking caution for abstinence till the
marriage be solemnised." The minutes of Kirk
Sessions show that, in numerous instances,
during the latter half of the seventeenth century,
such deposits were retained for the space
of nine calendar months after the marriage.
The Kilmarnock Kirk Session was not so
strict. It was there ordered, in 1670, that the

deposit should be returned to the parties on the expiration of half a year. Whatever the term was, if scandal arose before it expired, the deposit became forfeited.

Kirk Sessions in some cases accepted personal security in lieu of cash, the bondsmen in such cases becoming liable in the event of scandal arising, or the non-solemnisation of the marriage. But this system, so convenient for those who could not raise the caution money, or "pawn," as it was commonly called, was in course of time abandoned. The Kirk Session of Mauchline instructed the clerk, in 1691, "to take neither bond nor cautioner for consignation money, but to require that the money be laid down, to remain in his hand for the space of three-quarters of a year." The example was followed by other Kirk Sessions, but the custom continued for a long time afterwards, and was never formally abolished, falling into abeyance gradually. Dr Edgar, in his "Old Church Life in Scotland," states that "on a page at the end of a small volume of scroll minutes still extant there is a writing, under date 23rd November, 1771, which has all the appearance of being a genuine matrimonial consignation bond."

The First Book of Discipline makes it peremptory that no persons should be married without the consent of the parents, unless it should appear that there was no reasonable ground for the refusal of their consent. The Westminster Directory qualifies this by ruling that the consent of parents should be obtained to first marriages, especially if the parties were under age. It is not clear whether non-age means under the age of twenty-one, or is to be interpreted by the decree of the General Assembly of 1600 that, "considering that there is no statute of the kirk, . . . defining the age of persons which are to be married, ordain that no minister within this realm presume to join in matrimony any persons in time coming, except the man be fourteen years of age, and the woman twelve complete." The same ages are given in the First Book of Discipline.

Deviations from even this rule sometimes occurred, and may be classed among the permitted irregularities referred to at the beginning of this paper. The marriage of heiresses under the age of twelve was not infrequent, the plea of the guardians, that they feared the abduction of their wards if longer unmarried, being admitted.

There is a record of the marriage of a girl in her eleventh year to a boy of fourteen in 1659; and no longer ago than 1859 a girl was married at Edinburgh, who was entered by the registrar as in her eleventh year.   The official inspector thought there must have been an error in the registration, but inquiry proved that the entry was correct.

There was no laxity, however, in the matter of prohibited degrees of relationship.   In 1731, an irregular marriage came before the Presbytery of Ayr.   The banns had been forbidden on the ground that the woman's first husband had been grand-uncle to the second bridegroom.   The lovers thereupon proceeded to Carlisle, and were there united in marriage.   The Presbytery pronounced them guilty of incest, prohibited them from cohabitation, and the interdict being disregarded, passed sentence of excommunication.

Marriage might be refused in former times when either of the parties was found to be "under scandal."   In 1565, the General Assembly enacted that "such as lie in sin under promise of marriage, deferring the solemnisation, should satisfy publicly, in the place of repentance, upon the Lord's day before they be married."

Many instances are recorded of persons appearing before the Kirk Session, and denying upon
oath that they had committed the sin of which
they were accused. The Kirk Sessions were
equally diligent in their endeavours to prevent
scandals. In 1621, it was reported to the Kirk
Session of Perth "that Janet Watson holds
house by herself, where she may give occasion
of slander," wherefore an elder was directed "to
admonish her in the Session's name either to
marry or to pass to service."

But while the Church authorities were so
zealous for the morals of the nation and the
prevention of scandal, they appear to have sometimes thrown impediments in the way of lawful
marriage. In the early years following the
Reformation, it was a very frequent ordinance of
Kirk Sessions that no persons should be allowed
to marry until they were able to repeat to the
minister or reader the Lord's Prayer, the Apostles'
Creed, and the Ten Commandments. Either a
"pawn" was required for the fulfilment of this
condition or a fine was exacted in case of failure.
In some parishes the Kirk Sessions went beyond
this requirement, and insisted on regular attendance at public worship. In 1700, the Kirk

Session of Galston, "considering that there were some who lived within the parish who did not join with the congregation in public worship, nor submit themselves to discipline, and yet craved common privileges of members of this congregation, such as proclamation in order to marriage, concluded that none such should have privileges, until they should engage to live orderly for the time to come." And a further entry, of the same date, states that one of the persons referred to applied for proclamation of banns, and, on the resolution being communicated to him, he "engaged, through God's grace, to live orderly, and to wait upon gospel ordinances more particularly, and was then allowed to be proclaimed."

There was some difference of opinion in the early days of the Reformed Church as to whether a pre-contract should be an impediment to marriage with another person. The minutes of the Westminster Assembly show that some of the divines maintained that a promise of marriage was a "covenant of God," and could not be broken, even by mutual consent. The Church of Scotland did not adopt this view. In 1570, the General Assembly directed that persons desiring to withdraw from a contract of

marriage should, if nothing had followed, be
allowed to do so.   In the same year, an appeal
was made to the Assembly from the decision of
a Kirk Session that a man should not be allowed
to marry any woman other than a former servant
of the appellant, whom he had seduced.   He
had applied to the Kirk Session for proclamation
of banns, putting in the document known as a
"discharge of marriage," signed by the woman
he had wronged, for three or four successive
years, but it was persistently refused recognition.
The Assembly sustained his appeal, gave him
the liberty he sought, and added, "yea, and there
is injury done to him already."

Sometimes, however, contracted persons declined to set each other free, and forbade the
publication of banns with any other person.
In 1689, one John Meikle was cited to appear
before the Presbytery of Ayr, to show cause why
he forbade the banns of Janet Campbell.   He
pleaded that Janet had been engaged to him,
and on that ground he objected to her becoming
the wife of any other man.   The Presbytery
decided that Janet was free to do so.   In 1777,
a woman applied to the Kirk Session of Mauchline to have her banns stopped, on the ground

that she had changed her mind, and had become engaged to another man. The first lover opposed the application, pleading that she was his "by the covenant of God." The Kirk Session did not admit his plea. The publication of banns was stopped, and a minute of the Session justifies this decision, on the ground that "there would be an obvious impropriety in proceeding further in the proclamation, after being certified by the woman of her resolution not to marry the petitioner."

There were some superstitions connected with marriage as to lucky and unlucky days and seasons. Perthshire couples refrained from wedlock in January, and everywhere it was declined in May. In the Lowlands, Friday was considered an unlucky day for weddings, but in the Highlands, it was the day generally chosen for the ceremony. These notions had no weight with the compilers of the First Book of Discipline, who expressed their opinion that Sunday was the day "most expedient." On the other hand, the Westminster Assembly advised that marriages should not be solemnised on the Lord's day. The latter may have been influenced by the same reason that moved the

Kirk Session of Perth to adopt, in 1584, a
resolution that " forasmuch as sundry poor desire
to, because they have not to buy clothes, nor
to make bridals, marriages should be as well
celebrated on Thursday, within our Parish
Kirk in time of sermon, as on Sunday." The
former, on the other hand, probably had in
view the disorderly scenes to which a wedding
was often the prelude. The General Assembly,
in 1645, adopted the view of the Westminster
Directory, and marriages from that date were
generally solemnised on the day of the weekly
lecture.

In former times, and down to the first quarter
of the present century, the celebration of a
marriage otherwise than in church was regarded
as irregular and clandestine. In 1581, the
General Assembly "concluded by common consent of the whole brethren, that in times coming
no marriage be celebrated, nor sacraments administered, in private houses." At that time,
and long afterwards, ministers were liable to
deposition, and were actually deposed, for marrying persons in private houses. It is a fact,
nevertheless, that though the law of the Church
remains as settled in 1581, marriages celebrated

in private houses have not been regarded as irregular since the beginning of the last century; and the records of the General Sessions of Edinburgh show that, as long ago as 1643, private marriages were not infrequent in that city, where, however, they were restricted to the well-to-do classes by a fine of twenty marks.

Weddings were usually followed by great festivities, which were generally on a scale so extensive, and carried to so great an excess, that the records of Kirk Sessions during the seventeenth century show numerous regulations for their restriction. They fixed the number of guests who might be lawfully entertained on such occasions, and the hour at which the festivities should cease. Many of the customs observed were peculiar to the country, or to certain parts of it. In the Highlands, until about a century ago, the bride walked round the wedding party at the close of the ceremony, saluting each with a kiss. A dish was then passed round, in which each deposited a coin, the amount collected being given to the bride. The term "penny wedding" appears to have arisen from this custom. Owing to the large number of guests entertained, which Kirk

Sessions did not venture to reduce to less than forty, it was usual for the neighbours to assist in providing for them. Landowners gave beef, mutton and venison ; farmers, poultry and dairy produce ; and the minister and the schoolmaster lent cooking utensils. The bridal feast was followed by a dance.

Some peculiar rites, of ancient and pagan origin, were practised at the home-coming of the bride. The guests assembled at the door, on the threshold of which a sieve containing bread and cheese was held over her head, and, as she entered the house, a cake of shortbread was broken over her head, the young folk present scrambling for the fragments. The ceremony was completed by the bride sweeping the hearth with a broom.

This paper would not be complete without some notice of an aspect of the matter with which it deals, which has not received the attention to which it is certainly entitled. The law relating to marriage remains unsettled. It has been so constantly regarded as a matter for ecclesiastical regulation, that it has been practically left to be dealt with by Presbyteries and Kirk Sessions. "As far back as any living man remembers," says Dr Edgar, " it has taken very few formalities to constitute in Scotland a marriage that is binding in law. A man and a woman have only had to take up house together, and declare themselves husband and wife. The law thereupon pronounced them married persons. But this was not always understood to be the law of the land in Scotland, and the Church of Scotland did not always recognise such unions as marriages." But while writing of what was or was not *understood* to be the law, he tells us nothing as to what the law really was or is.

It seems to have been the practice of the Church, in former times, to pronounce her own judgment, and then to ask the State to confirm it. In the first General Assembly held in Scotland, that of 1560, there was a declaration made concerning marriages within certain degrees of relationship, and " the authority of the Estates was craved to be interposed to that finding as the law." There were many of the ministers of the Reformed Church who held that a religious ceremony was not necessary to constitute a valid marriage. One of the members of the Westminster Assembly, in 1644, expressed the opinion, previously given by Luther, that only the consent of the parties was necessary. This view appears to have prevailed very generally among the laity, notwithstanding the action taken so frequently by Kirk Sessions in opposition to it.

The question continued to be disputed throughout the last century. Writers on legal questions held one view, and judges on the bench pronounced contrariwise. Erskine argued that, in Scotland, the consent of the parties was all that was necessary to constitute a valid marriage. Lord Braxfield affirmed the opposite in 1796. Lord Fraser, on a later occasion, said that the view set forth by Erskine was never judicially pronounced to be the law of Scotland until 1811. Can we wonder, therefore, when lawyers and judges disagree, at the haziness of mental vision displayed by Kirk Sessions, and the frequent want of uniformity in their decisions?

Gretna Green Gossip.

GRETNA GREEN is the name of an in-
significant village in the Border country
between England and Scotland. It is situated
in Dumfriesshire, near the mouth of the Esk,
nine miles north-west of Carlisle, and consequently within a mile of the English border.
Probably no place of such absence of pretension
to size and population has attained the notoriety
which attaches to the name of Gretna Green, a
distinction it has obtained merely through its
being the first place suitable for stoppage after
the English border was once passed. This
close proximity was utilised by runaway couples,
who, dispensing, for various reasons, with the
preliminaries of anyone's consent to their union,
or the publication of banns requisite by the
English Marriage Laws, could, when once on
Scottish ground, accomplish their wedding by
simply declaring before witnesses their mutual
willingness to undertake the contract. To the

facility, then, which the Marriage Laws of
Scotland offered to amorous and impatient
couples (minors or not), the fisher-village of
Gretna Green owes its repute as a chosen altar
of Hymen. A marriage once declared here
was henceforward considered valid, and after
exchanging before any witness the mutual
promises, the pair might return to England at
once, the knot being tied beyond all chance of
dispute. As might be expected, haste was a
great factor in these summary pairings, and
consequently postillions were largely employed
to get over the distance between Carlisle and
Gretna, a course upon which, no doubt, many a
tough race has been run between prudent parent
or guardian and ardent runaways.

The "parsons" of Gretna were the ordinary
inhabitants, who were weavers, fishermen (Gretna
being at the head of the Solway), blacksmiths,
&c., and their fees were entirely arbitrary, being
fixed on the spot, according to the private
information of the postillions, or according to the
appearance and simplicity of the young couple.
Marriages have been contracted here for a glass
of whisky, while on the other hand a fee of
twenty pounds has been paid, as in the case of

Lord Chief Justice Erskine, who availed himself of the easy ceremony, and even much larger sums, as in the cases of the Earl of Westmoreland, Lord Deerhurst, and others, who paid to the officiating "cleric" upwards of one hundred guineas. In the absence of any local person to receive the attestations to the contract, the postillions themselves have been known to assume the sacerdotal functions.

The first broker in Gretna Green marriages was one Scott, who lived at a point called the Rigg, a few miles from the village. It is said that he commenced his infamous profession about the year 1750, but beyond the fact that he was a crafty fellow, who could turn the emergencies of the time to his own advantage, little is known of him. The next who undertook the remunerative duties of high priest was George Gordon, an old soldier, who invariably wore as canonicals a full military uniform of a by-gone type—a tremendous cocked-hat, scarlet coat, and jackboots, with a ponderous sword dangling from his belt. His "church," which had the appearance of a barn, stood a little to the left of the public road; his altar was an ale cask upon which was placed an open Bible. Following Gordon, Joseph Paisley (sometimes called Pasley) became the recognised parson. He was a fisherman, who agreeably united with the duties of that position the pursuits of smuggler and tobacconist. He has been also called a blacksmith, but this was simply a fanciful allusion to the part he took in the Gretna Green marriages, Vulcan being the marriage maker of the gods as well as their smith. He commenced the matrimonial business in 1789, and from being retiring in his manner of dealing, became audaciously unscrupulous, going so far even as to supply fictitious signatures to the certificates, instead of, as at first, resorting to the less culpable proceeding of signing his own name as a witness. It is said of this man that at his death, about 1811, he weighed twenty-five stones. He was a coarse, blatant individual, and habitually appeared in a sort of priestly dress, even in his constant dissipations. At his death the priesthood was taken by his son-in-law, Robert Elliott, who kept an account of his transactions, and afterwards published them under the title of "The Gretna Green Memoirs." In this he states that between 1811 and 1839, not less than 7744 persons were united by him at Gretna. The *Times*, in a review of the book, doubted the

accuracy of the assertion, which drew from him a
reply in the form of a letter to that paper. He
said, " I can show registers for that number from
my commencement, and which either you or any
respectable individual may inspect here, and
which I can substantiate on oath."

We give here an extract from the " Memoirs "
of Elliott.   He says :—" As the marriage ceremony performed by me and my predecessors may
be interesting to many of my readers, I give
it verbatim :   The parties are first asked their
names and places of abode ;   they are then
asked to stand up, and inquired of if they are
both single persons ;   if the answer be in the
affirmative, the ceremony proceeds.   Each is
next asked, ' Did you come here of your own
free will and accord ? '   Upon receiving an affirmative answer, the priest commences filling in the
printed form of the certificate.   The man is
then asked, ' Do you take this woman to be your
lawful wedded wife, forsaking all others, and
keep to her as long as you both shall live ? '   He
answers, ' I will.'   The woman is asked the same
question, when, being answered the same, the
woman then produces a ring, which she gives to
the man, who hands it to the priest ; the priest

then returns it to the man, and orders him to put it on the fourth finger of the woman's left hand, repeating these words, 'With this ring I thee wed, with my body I thee worship, with all my goods I thee endow, in the name of the Father, Son, and Holy Ghost. Amen.' They then take hold of each other's right hand, and the woman says, 'What God joins together let no man put asunder.' Then the priest says, 'Forasmuch as this man and this woman have come together by giving and receiving a ring, I therefore declare them to be man and wife before God and these witnesses, in the name of the Father, Son, and Holy Ghost. Amen.'"

The following are among the memorable matches effected through the agency of Robert Elliott, and recorded in his Memoirs :—

1812.—Rev. Wm. Freemantle, an English clergyman. C. Ewen Law, son of Lord Ellenborough, to Miss Nightingale.

1815.—A "droll gaberlunzie without legs or arms, to a comely damsel, both appearing anxious for the ceremony," to the disgust of the not too fastidious parson himself.

1816.—Lord Chief Justice Erskine. Within a year, however, his lordship unsuccessfully tried

to loosen his matrimonial chains by a divorce by
the Scottish law.

1826.—E. Gibbon Wakefield, with Miss
Turner. Of the trial which ensued upon this
union we give particulars below.

During the latter part of Elliott's "ministration" competition in the marrying business
became brisk, and he had numerous rivals, the
most powerful of these candidates for clerical
emolument being another son of Mars, named
David Laing. The competition became so pronounced that the rival parsons canvassed for the
assistance and co-operation of the postillions, who,
commencing by receiving a commission per runaway pair, at last ended by working upon a
system of equal shares with their priestly co-
partners.

In 1827, at the Kent Assizes, a Gretna Green
marriage was the subject of a curious trial before
Mr Baron Hullock. The action was taken
against one Mrs Wakefield and her two sons,
for conspiring "to take away by subtle strata-
gems" a young lady named Turner, who had
not yet left school. The David Laing above
mentioned was called as a witness on behalf of
the defendants, and he affirmed that the couple

were married lawfully according to the Scottish fashion—namely, by putting on the lady's finger a ring. The witness said he was seventy-five years old, and had spent more than half of his life in the performance of marriages. In cross-examination by Mr Brougham, he admitted obtaining £30 for this particular ceremony, or even £50, but could not remember exactly, "being somewhat hard of hearing." The accused was found guilty of causing this young lady to "contract matrimony without the consent of her father, and to the great disparagement of the King's peace." The chief prisoner, E. Gibbon Wakefield, was convicted of abduction, and the marriage, which excited considerable public attention, was afterwards rendered invalid, and annulled by an Act of Parliament specially obtained. After this flagrant case Gretna Green marriages fell into disrepute, and the business showed a steady decline, though cases of the employment of pseudo-parsons are on much later record. In 1853, a person named Thomas Blythe, a witness before the Court of Probate at Westminster, stated that he lived at Springfield, Gretna Green, and that he obtained his livelihood by means of agriculture, but that he not unfrequently took advantage of opportunities to increase his income by small strokes of business in the "joining" line. Again, the demise of another "joiner" was announced so late as 1872, when the obituary of Simon Laing appeared in the *Glasgow Herald*. It is probable, however, that the pursuit of his "clerical" profession ceased long before the date of his death, for, in 1856, the old law by which the mere verbal declaration of consent before witnesses was sufficient to constitute a Scottish legal marriage became effete through the passing of the Act of Parliament, 19 and 20 Victoria, cap. 96. By this Act the laws of Scotland and England were brought into assimilation, and in that year the occupation of the northern hedge-parsons was virtually gone.

It may be said such marriages as those we have described were considered as clandestine and ill-advised in Scotland, as in more southern parts, the Church of Scotland doing all that lay in its power to discourage and prevent them. The only punishment, however, which it had for transgressors being excommunication, the restraint by the Kirk was very slight, its injunctions and fulminary condemnations being treated with contempt.

Probably the best known of the notable marriages which have taken place at Gretna is that of the Earl of Westmoreland with the daughter of Child, the banker, whose counting-house was at the sign of the Marygold, in the Strand. The romantic but determined couple had the advantage of an early start, one starlight night in May, but the pursuit was not less hot than the departure had been well arranged, and when within a few miles of the Border the coach was nearly overtaken by Mr Child's carriage. The Earl, however, not to be baulked when so near the end of the journey, shot down one of the pursuing horses, while one of the servants cut the carriage straps behind. The crown of firs which mark Gretna from the surrounding country came quickly into view, the bridge was crossed, and the village was reached by the reckless couple. A parson was found, and quickly the Earl and Miss Child were made one. Within a year Mr Child died, it is said, of the mortification and disappointment connected with this affair. The elder daughter of the match, Lady Sophia Fane, afterwards married Lord Jersey, and inherited his immense fortune, including Child's Bank at Temple Bar.

Death and Burial Customs and Superstitions.

A MONG the many pagan beliefs and observ-
ances which were adhered to during many
centuries of Christian creed and worship, and
some of which have survived among the less
enlightened even to the present day, a large
place is held by those connected with death
and burial. In Scotland, many trivial things
were regarded as omens of death. In the
northern Highlands, an itching of the nose was
believed to prognosticate the death of a neigh-
bour. In the southern parts, a humming in the
ear was held to prelude the death of a relative.
The crowing of a cock at an unusual hour
was regarded as a token of the death of some
person in the parish. In the Lowlands, the
howling of a strange dog was accepted as a
warning of the approaching death of some
inmate of the house near which the melancholy
wail was raised. The "death candle," as the
phosphoric light sometimes seen flickering over

burial-grounds was called, was similarly regarded in the Hebrides.

In some parts of the Highlands it is still believed that the last moments of a dying person are prolonged by the door of the death-chamber being closed. It is usual, therefore, for it to be left ajar, so that there may be room for the departing spirit to take its flight, and yet the intrusion of any evil thing be prevented. When a death occurred, the clock was stopped, and its face covered, as were all the mirrors in the house. A bell was laid under the head of the corpse, and a vessel containing earth and salt placed upon the breast.

From the moment of death until the departure of the funeral procession to the place of burial, the corpse was watched night and day by parties of friends and neighbours, who relieved each other. Silence was observed, but this did not prevent the consumption of much ale and whisky. Among the poorer classes the interment took place soon after death, in order to lessen the cost of watching, but the well-to-do deferred the funeral for at least a week, and sometimes a fortnight, in order that the hospitality of the house might be more extensively offered and enjoyed. Among these a feast was given on the evening preceding the funeral.

There were many superstitious beliefs and customs connected with funerals. As in England, the proverb was accepted that "happy is the corpse that the rain falls on." If the funeral party, on the way to the burial-ground, walked in a straggling manner, it was regarded as an omen that another death would soon occur under the same roof. In the Hebrides, if one of the party stumbled and fell, the incident was held to indicate that he would be the next to die.

In the last century, there was a lamentable amount of ale and whisky drinking before and after funerals. The company began to assemble two hours before the time appointed for the corpse to be carried from the house. If the deceased was a farmer, each of the guests was offered a glass of whisky at the gate of the farm-yard, and another on crossing the threshold. On entering the guest-room, a portion of short-bread and another glass of whisky were handed to him, a reverential silence being observed for a time, after which conversation was carried on in whispers. When all the guests were assembled, the minister commenced a religious service, which lasted about three-quarters of an hour. This was followed by the handing round of oatcake, cheese, and whisky, and afterwards shortbread and more whisky. Then the coffin was carried out, and followed to the grave by all those who were sufficiently sober to walk straight.

Religious ceremonies at burials have never found favour in the Church of Scotland. They were discouraged both by the First Book of Discipline and the Westminster Directory, the compilers of the former saying, " for avoiding all inconveniences, we judge it best that neither singing nor reading be at the burial, . . . yea, without all kind of ceremony heretofore used, other than that the dead be committed to the grave with such gravity and sobriety as those that be present may seem to fear the judgment of God, and to hate sin, which is the cause of death." The Westminster Directory deals with the matter in much the same way, the Assembly maintaining that the burial of the dead is not a part of the work of the ministry, as baptisms and marriages are.

It appears to have been customary in the early

centuries of the Church in Scotland, to bury the
dead uncoffined; and this custom prevailed
among the poor for some time after the Reformation. It lingered in rural districts longer
than in towns, and in some later than in others;
but the Kirk Session records of some parishes
refer to the provision of coffins for the interment
of persons who were practically paupers in the
last quarter of the seventeenth century. As to
the mode of burial before the use of coffins
became general, the General Assembly ordained,
in 1563, " that a bier should be made in every
country parish, to carry the dead corpse of the
poor to the burial-place, and that those of the
villages or houses next adjacent to the house
where the dead corpse lieth, or a certain number
out of every house, shall convey the dead corpse
to the burial-place, and bury it six feet under the
earth."

The biers appear to have been of more than
one kind. Some of them were mere rails upon
which the corpse was laid, covered only with a
pall, called in Scotland a mort-cloth. Others
were wooden boxes, with the lid on one side
furnished with a hinge, so that the corpse could
be taken out, and lowered into the grave by

ropes.   In some parts of the Highlands, a long
basket, made of twisted rushes, was used, and
called the "death hamper."   There were three
pairs of loop handles, through which short iron
bars were passed for convenience of carriage ;
and on the grave being reached, it was lowered
by ropes, so arranged that it could be turned
over and recovered for future use.

Before the Reformation, it was the custom to
bury unbaptised children apart from members of
the Church, the north side of the churchyard
being reserved for that purpose.   This was
afterwards regarded as contrary to the true
principles of Protestantism, and in 1641 the
Synod of Fife ordained that "all these who
superstitiously carries the dead about the kirk
before burial, also these who bury unbaptised
bairns apart, be taken notice of and censured."
Suicides and excommunicated persons were also,
at one time, buried apart, and at night.   In 1582,
the Kirk Session of Perth refused to allow the
corpse of a man who had committed suicide by
drowning to be "brought through the town in
daylight, neither yet to be buried among the
faithful, . . . but in the little Inch within the
water."

With regard to interment within the churches, the Scottish Reformers seem to have been in advance of those south of the Border. The Brownists were as much in advance of the former, for in 1590 one of the leaders of that denomination wrote :—" Where learned you to bury in hallowed churches and churchyards, as though you had no fields to bury in ? Methinks the churchyards, of all other places, should be not the convenientest for burial ; it was a thing never used till Popery began, and it is neither comely nor wholesome." Interment in churches was, on sanitary grounds, even more objectionable than in the grounds adjacent to them, and in 1576 the General Assembly prohibited the practice, and ordered that those who contravened the ordinance should be suspended from the privileges of the Church.

Long after that time, however, burials in churches continued to take place, owing to the value attached by families of rank above that of the commonalty to the privilege of having their relatives buried apart. In 1643, the Assembly again prohibited all persons, " of whatsoever quality, to bury any deceased person within the body of the kirk, where the people

meet for hearing of the Word." But the ordinance
was disregarded by all who thought themselves
powerful enough to do so, and as ministers had
very little to do with a matter which had been
declared to be unministerial, they usually found
their will sufficient to serve their purpose. In
1695, the Kirk Session of Kilmarnock recorded
a minute that, the north aisle being then filled
with pews, "they shall, when required, cause lift
six pews, on each end, next to the north wall of
the aisle, so oft as any of the families of Rowallan,
Craufordland, and Grange, shall have occasion to
bury their dead ; . . . and, after burial, the said
pews shall be set up again in their places, at the
expense of the session." Kirk Sessions seem
to have felt themselves powerless to enforce
their ordinances in the face of a long existing
custom and a fancied right of the gentry to
burial within the church ; and in one instance,
which occurred in a Highland parish in 1727,
the Kirk Session petitioned the Presbytery to
"put a stop to such a bad practice."

The custom of ringing a bell at funerals,
which was a common one before the Reformation,
was continued afterwards. There is an entry in
the records of Glasgow, for 1577, of the sale of

" the auld bell that yed throw the toun of auld at the burial of the dead." In 1621, the Kirk Session of Dumbarton ordained that " the beadle, John Tome, and his successors, shall ring the mort-bell before all persons deceased within town, for such prices as the minister and session shall set down." It may be that the custom, like the ringing of church bells, originated in the superstition that the sound of bells scared away evil spirits ; for an edict of the Town Council of Aberdeen, passed in 1643, includes the tolling and ringing of bells among the "superstitious rites used at funerals," which it prohibits.

Towards the close of the seventeenth century, it seems to have been usual for the church bell to be tolled at funerals, and that without any charge being made, for, in 1696, the Kirk Session of Mauchline made a minute that they " thought it reasonable that whoever desired the tolling of the bell at the funeral of their relations, should pay some small quantity of money to the kirk treasurer, to be disposed of for the poor's use." Similar ordinances were passed about the same time by the Kirk Sessions of other parishes in Ayrshire. It was decided, however, in the Civil Court, in

1730, that the money arising from fees for the
ringing of bells and burials within the church
did not properly belong to the fund for the relief
of the poor, but might be used for the mainten-
ance of the fabric of the church. The poor,
however, do not appear to have lost much by
this decision, for during the year ended October,
1732, the "big" bell at Kilmarnock was tolled
for funerals only seven times. It may be ex-
plained that there were two bells in many
churches, the larger one to be tolled at the
funerals of the rich, and the smaller at those
of the poor. In the register of burials at
Inverness, the words "big bells" are added to
the entries of the funerals of "persons of
quality."

The burials register of the parish of Tough,
in Aberdeenshire, record that, in 1784, forty-two
of the parishioners joined in the purchase of a
new bell for the church, stipulating that, when
deaths occurred in their families, "the bell be
rung once before the day of interment, that is,
when the officer gets the first notice of a con-
tributor's death, and then upon the day of
interment, from morning until the coffin be laid
in the ground, in the manner that bells ought

to be rung at funerals, and that by no other
person than the officer allenarlie."

Palls were, from a very early period, regarded
as essential parts of the funeral paraphernalia.
In 1598, the Kirk Session of Glasgow ordered
a black cloth to be bought "to be laid on the
corpses of the poor," and, for at least two hundred
years afterwards, it was the custom for the " mort-
cloth " to be taken to the house where a corpse
awaited burial, and laid over it. The reason for
this may be found in the early custom of burial
without a coffin, and in the case of those who
desired to show some regard for appearances, in
the proclamation of Council in 1684, that coffins
should not be covered with silk or decorated
with fringes or metal-work. The mort-cloths
kept "to be laid on the corpses of the poor"
were probably of coarse black woollen cloth ; but
those used at the funerals of well-to-do people
were, as a rule, of richer and more handsome
material. In the sessional records of the parish
of Mauchline for 1672 there is an entry of the
payment of a sum of no less than £10, 12s. 4d.
as completing the price of a new mort-cloth,
which implies that some portion of the total cost
had been paid previously. Another new mort-

cloth provided for the same parish in the last
quarter of the eighteenth century is described as
having been made of Genoa velvet, conformably
fringed.

The preaching of funeral sermons received
little favour in Scotland during the early period
of the Reformed Church. "We have," says
Baillie, writing from London during the sitting
of the Westminster Assembly, "with much
difficulty, passed a proposition for abolishing
their ceremonies at burials, but our difference
about funeral sermons seems irreconcilable. As
it has been here and everywhere preached, it
is nothing but an abuse of preaching, to serve
the humours only of rich people for a reward.
Our Church has expressly discharged them, on
many good reasons; it's here a good part of the
minister's livelihood, therefore they will not quit
it. After three days' debate, we cannot yet find
a way of agreeance."

It was in consequence of this inability to agree
on the subject that the Scottish commissioners
at Westminster declined to hear the sermon
preached on the occasion of the funeral of Pym.
Baillie wrote :—"On Wednesday, Mr Pym was
carried from his house to Westminster on the

shoulders, as the fashion is, of the chief men of the Lower House, all the House going in procession before him, and before them the Assembly of Divines. Marshall had a most eloquent and pertinent funeral sermon—which we would not hear, for funeral sermons we must have away, with the rest."

The earliest registers of deaths are those of Aberdeen, which commence in 1560; Perth, beginning in 1561, and the Canongate, Edinburgh, in 1565. The register of burials in the last-named parish commences in 1612, and that of Greyfriars in 1658. Those of rural parishes generally commence in the last century, and they are, as a rule, more or less imperfect. It appears from the Edinburgh registers, in which the deaths are summarised annually, that the mortality has greatly diminished during the last hundred and fifty years. In the first four decades of the last century, nearly two-thirds of the deaths were those of children, and the deaths of adult females were double those of adult males. The dawn of a better state of things appears in 1741, when the deaths of 276 men, 401 women, and 942 children, were registered, which, if we accept the generally received statement that the population of the city was then fifty thousand, gives an annual average death-rate of 34 per thousand. The average mortality of the ten years ending with 1878, as shown by the report of the Registrar General, was 24 per thousand; and that of the week ending October 8, 1898, was 20 per thousand; which was precisely that of the thirty - three largest towns of the southern portion of the island.

Contemporary events in other places were not unfrequently recorded in the local registers of deaths in the sixteenth and seventeenth centuries. Thus, in the Aberdeen register, we have the murder of Lord Darnley very circumstantially recorded as follows, though under a wrong date: —" The ninth [10th] day of February, the year of God 1566, Henry Stuart, Lord Darnley, King of Scotland, who married Mary Stuart, Queen of Scotland, daughter to King James the Fifth, was cruelly murdered under night, in Edinburgh, in the Cowgate, at the Kirk of Field, by James Hepburn, Earl of Bothwell, and other his assisters, whose deed God revenge. So be it." * The ascription of the crime to Bothwell

* The spelling of this and the following extracts is modernised.

does not appear in the Canongate register, which merely records the fact of Darnley being blown up with gunpowder.

The assassination of the Earl of Murray is recorded in several parish registers. The session clerk of Aberdeen recorded it, with much particularity, as follows :—" The twenty-third day of January, the year of God 1569, James, Earl of Murray, Lord Abernethy, Regent to the King and realm of Scotland, was cruelly murdered and shot in the town of Linlithgow, by a false traitor, James Hamilton of Bodywallhaucht, by the conspiracy and treason of his own servant, William Kircaldy, and John Hamilton, bloody Bishop of St. Andrew's, whose deed we pray God to revenge. So be it." With equal circumstantiality the same clerk made an entry in the register of the murder of Coligny, and the horrible massacre of the Protestants of Paris, on St. Bartholomew's day, 1572, which event he prays God to revenge.

Some of the entries in the church registers of Edinburgh are of considerable historical interest. In that of St. Giles is chronicled the removal of the remains of the Marquis of Montrose from the Abbey Church of Holyrood to St. Giles's

Church, where they were honoured with a magnificent and pompous funeral. The entry in the register of burials records the final interment as follows:—" 11 May 1661.—The Rt. Hon. James, Marquis of Montrose, Earl of Kincardine, Lord Grahame and Mugdok, His Majesty's late commissioner and Captain General for the kingdom of Scotland, and knt. of most hon. order of the Garter, was conveyed from the kirk of Holyrood House with great honour and solemnity to St. Giles's kirk and buried." The corpse had been, in the first instance, interred at the Burgh Muir, so that this was the third removal.

The register of the Greyfriars' Church, Edinburgh, contains the following record of another and more generally interesting translation: —" Robert Garvock, Patrick Forman, James Stewart, David Fernie, Alexander Russell, was executed in the Gallowlee, for owning the truth, upon the 10 day of October 1681 years, and their heads fixed upon Bristo Port, taken down and buried privately in Louristone Yards, now accidentally dug up upon the 15 day of October 1726, and buried decently upon the 19 day of the said month in the Greyfriars' churchyard, close to the Martyrs' Tomb."

The grandeur of the final interment of the remains of the Marquis of Montrose, followed later by the costly obsequies of Lord Roslin, induced the Scottish Parliament, in 1681, to pass an Act which, besides restricting the number of persons who might attend the funeral of a person of rank to one hundred, prohibited "the using or carrying of any branches, banners, and other honours at church, except only the eight branches to be upon the pall, or upon the coffin where there is no pall." The Act seems, however, to have had little effect in diminishing the excessive costliness of funerals among all classes above the very poorest. The funeral of Sir William Hamilton, who died in 1707, was attended with a display and an amount of hospitality which cost a sum equal to two years of his salary as a judge. The funeral of Lachlan Macintosh, chief of the Highland clan of that name, in 1736, cost (including the customary festivities) a sum which involved his successors in pecuniary embarrassments for a century afterwards. The funerals of Highland chiefs were attended by all the clan, sometimes numbering thousands of persons, and the procession to the place of burial extending to more than a mile in length ; the coronach—a hymn of lamentation, an example of which may be found in Scott's " Lady of the Lake "—being chanted by hundreds of voices, accompanied by the bagpipes.

The Story of a Stool.

JAMES I. after the Reformation introduced
into Scotland bishops, and his son Charles I.
attempted to force upon the Scottish church
a book of canons and a liturgy. Both actions
were regarded with strong aversion, and cul-
minated in bitter strife. The king directed
that on Sunday, July 23rd, 1637, the new
service-book should be read in every parish
church in Scotland. Before the appointed day
arrived, opposition was manifest in all quarters,
and few had the courage, even if they had the
desire, to conduct their services from the new
prayer-book.

On the eventful Sunday when the new order
of service was to be formally introduced, the
chief church of the capital of Scotland, the old
Cathedral of St. Giles, was filled by an unusually
large congregation. Among those present were
two archbishops, several bishops, the lords
chancellor and treasurer, privy council, judges,
and magistrates. A large number of the humble

people, composed chiefly of the wives of citizens and their maids, filled the body of the church. In those days no pews were in the church, and the poor-folk brought clasp-stools.

When Dean Hannay, attired in a surplice, commenced reading prayers from the service-book a riot arose which has seldom been equalled in the house of God. The Dean could not be heard for the clamour of many voices. The voice of a female—that of Jenny Geddes—was heard above others. She cried, " Out, out! does the false loon mean to say his black mass at my lug?" and then threw her stool at the Dean's head.

This was the signal for a riot: an attempt was made to tear from the Dean his surplice, but he disengaged himself from it, and with difficulty made his escape. Hand-clapping, hisses, curses, &c., put an end to any attempt to conduct the service. The Bishop of Edin-burgh attempted from the pulpit to restore order, but a stool was thrown at him, and, had not a friendly hand averted its course, doubtless he would have been seriously injured, or even killed. Stones and other missiles were thrown at the pulpit.

The Lord Chancellor, it is recorded, commanded the magistrates to call out the town-
guard to drive the ringleaders from the church.
The church was cleared of the rioters, but
outside they battered the doors, broke the
windows, cried out, " A Pope ! A Pope ! "
" Antichrist ! " " Stone him ! Stone him ! "   The

JENNY GEDDES' STOOL.

From the Antiquarian Museum, Edinburgh.

Dean tried to resume his reading, but the
shouts of the multitude without drowned his
voice.

The service in Greyfriars' Church had to be
stopped on account of the rioting without, and
at the college, we are told in Stevenson's
" Annals of Edinburgh," the minister preferred
the old extempore form of prayer, till he learned

R

how the liturgy had been received in other city churches.

On leaving church the Bishop of Edinburgh was attacked by the mob, and narrowly escaped death at their hands. Other rioting occurred, and for many years the memorable day was known as " Stony Sabbath."

The local authorities, it is recorded, desired to maintain order, and on the Monday the local magistrates repaired to a meeting of the Privy Council, and expressed their great regret at the outrage, and promised to discover the ringleaders and have them punished.

On one of the piers of St. Giles' Cathedral, Edinburgh, is a memorial brass bearing the following inscription :—

TO

JAMES HANNAY, D.D.,

DEAN OF THIS CATHEDRAL,

1634-1639.

He was the first and last who read the service-book in this church.

THIS MEMORIAL IS ERECTED IN HAPPIER TIMES BY HIS DESCENDANT.

In the Moray or south-west aisle is a memorial of gun-metal to Jenny Geddes, with an inscrip-

tion written by the late Lord President Inglis,
which reads as follows :—

CONSTANT ORAL TRADITION
AFFIRMS THAT NEAR THIS SPOT
A BRAVE SCOTCH WOMAN, JANET GEDDES,
ON THE 23 JULY 1637,
STRUCK THE FIRST BLOW IN THE GREAT STRUGGLE
FOR FREEDOM OF CONSCIENCE,
WHICH AFTER A CONFLICT OF HALF-A-CENTURY
ENDED IN THE ESTABLISHMENT
OF CIVIL AND RELIGIOUS LIBERTY.

IN the capital of Scotland are more imposing monuments than the Covenanters' Memorial in Greyfriars' Churchyard, but not one more historically interesting. It attracts the attention of visitors from all parts of the world, and to the inhabitants of the city it must be a matter of pride to have this memorial to the memory of the men who fought for religious freedom.

The early Scottish reformers were in earnest respecting their faith; a bond was prepared, setting forth that they would stand unflinchingly by the Calvinistic faith, and if necessary would fight in its defence.

This was signed on December 3rd, 1557, by the Earls of Glencairn, Argyll, and Morton, Lord Lorn, Erskine of Dun and many more, who assumed the title of "Lords of the Congregation."

A man in Scotland might do many indiscreet things and even be guilty of crime, and be pardoned; but to flinch or fall from the Covenant was to commit a sin that his countrymen could not forgive.

Charles I., aided by Archbishop Laud, attempted to force upon the Presbyterians of Scotland a liturgy, and in other ways to alter the mode of divine worship in the country. The king's action was regarded with alarm, and steps were taken to maintain the religious freedom of the country. The Solemn League and Covenant of 1557 against Popery was renewed and new articles added. A copy was sent to each town in Scotland. That belonging to Edinburgh was, on March 1st, 1638, solemnly read aloud in Greyfriars' churchyard. It was subscribed to by a large number of the nobility, gentry and others of all ranks and conditions, ages and sexes. It is impossible to count the signatures on the document, but it is believed that over five thousand names occur, and the more zealous added to their subscription such sentences as "till death." The size of the parchment is four feet long and three feet eight inches broad, and it is preserved in the Register Office, Edinburgh. It was spread upon a flat stone in the churchyard for signature, and was signed by all who could get near to it.

Not a few who signed this document were amongst the many who suffered death for their adherence to the faith they held. At the Battle of Bothwell Bridge on June 22nd, 1679, it is recorded that 800 Covenanters were slain on the field of battle, and about 1300 taken prisoners and brought to Edinburgh, and later 200 were conveyed to Stirling.

At Edinburgh the prisoners were kept in an enclosed piece of land (now forming a part of the graveyard of Greyfriars), in a great measure without shelter, for five months, and supported with a short supply of bread and water. Guards watched them day and night. The condition of the prisoners was most distressing and moved to pity the inhabitants of the city, but they were not permitted to render the least assistance.

The troubles of many of these brave men did not end with imprisonment. "On the 15th of November," it is recorded, "256 were taken to Leith and put on board a vessel to be carried to the plantations in America. The vessel sailed on the 27th, but was wrecked on the coast of Orkney on December 10th, when upwards of 200 perished. Some of the remaining prisoners were tried, condemned and executed; the remainder, upon signing bonds, obtained their liberty."

The monument is erected near the graves of the martyrs who were buried in Greyfriars' churchyard. It was in that part of the burial-ground that criminals were interred, and an allusion is made to this fact in the inscription on the martyrs' monument.

James Currie of Pentland obtained from the Town Council of Edinburgh, on August 28th, 1706, permission to erect a stone in Greyfriars' churchyard to the memory of the martyrs, on condition "there being no inscription to be put upon the tomb but the sixth chapter of Revelation, verses 9, 10 and 11."

A carved stone representing an open Bible, with the verses cut in full, was erected, and this forms, we are told, the under part of the present more stately monument, which was substituted in 1771, when the original slab was removed. The old inscription with some slight alterations was transferred to the present monument. The inscription is as follows :—

> " Halt, passenger, take heed what you do see.
> This tomb doth shew for what some men did die.
> Here lies interr'd the dust of those who stood
> 'Gainst perjury, resisting unto blood ;

Adhering to the covenants and laws ;
Establishing the same : which was the cause
Their lives were sacrific'd unto the lust
Of prelatists abjur'd ; though here their dust
Lies mixt with murderers and other crew,
Whom justice justly did to death pursue.
But as for them, no cause was to be found
Worthy of death ; but only they were found
Constant and steadfast, zealous, witnessing
For the prerogatives of Christ their King ;
Which truths were seal'd by famous Guthrie's head,
And all along to Mr Renwick's blood :
They did endure the wrath of enemies :
Reproaches, torments, deaths and injuries.
But yet they're those, who from such troubles came,
And now triumph in glory with the Lamb.

"From May 27th, 1661, that the most noble Marquis of
Argyle was beheaded, to the 17th February 1688, that Mr
James Renwick suffered, were one way or other murdered
and destroyed for the same cause about eighteen thousand, of
whom were executed at Edinburgh about an hundred of
noblemen, gentlemen, ministers and others, noble martyrs for
JESUS CHRIST. The most of them lie here.

Rev. vi. 9.—And when he had opened the fifth seal, I saw
     under the altar the souls of them that were slain
     for the word of God, and for the testimony which
     they held :

     10.—And they cried with a loud voice, saying, How
     long, O Lord, holy and true, dost thou not judge
     and avenge our blood on them that dwell on the
     earth ?

     11.—And white robes were given unto every one of
     them ; and it was said unto them that they should

THE MARTYRS' MONUMENT, EDINBURGH.

rest yet for a little season, until their fellow-servants also and their brethren, that should be killed as they were, should be fulfilled.

Chap. vii. 14.—These are they which came out of great tribulation, and have washed their robes and made them white in the blood of the Lamb.

Chap. ii. 10.—Be thou faithful unto death, and I will give thee a crown of life.

"The above monument was first erected by JAMES CURRIE, merchant, Pentland, and others, in 1706; renewed in 1771."

(Added on the monument at a subsequent date):—

"Yes, though the sceptic's tongue deride
Those martyrs who for conscience died—
Though modern history blight their fame,
And sneering courtiers hoot the name
Of men who dared alone be free,
Amidst a nation's slavery ;—
Yet long for them the poet's lyre
Shall wake its notes of heavenly fire ;
Their names shall nerve the patriot's hand
Upraised to save a sinking land ;
And piety shall learn to burn
With holier transports o'er their urn.

JAMES GRAHAME.

Peace to their mem'ry ! let no impious breath
Sell their fair fame, or triumph o'er their death.
Let Scotia's grateful sons their tear-drops shed,
Where low they lie in honour's gory bed ;
Rich with the spoil their glorious deeds had won,
And purchas'd freedom to a land undone—
A land which owes its glory and its worth
To those whom tyrants banish'd from the earth."

"For the accomplishment of this resolution, the three
kingdoms lie under no small debt of gratitude to the
Covenanters.   They suffered and bled both in fields and on
scaffolds for the cause of civil and religious liberty ; and shall
we reap the fruit of their sufferings, their prayers and their
blood, and yet treat their memory either with indifference or
scorn ?   No ! whatever minor faults may be laid to their
charge, whatever trivial accusations may be brought against
them, it cannot but be acknowledged that they were the
men who, 'singly and alone,' stood forward in defence of
Scotland's dearest rights, and to whom we at the present day
owe everything that is valuable to us either as men or as
Christians."

It only remains for us to add that James
Currie, who was the means of raising the original
monument, suffered much during the persecution
and more than once narrowly escaped capture.

INDEX

LIST OF PUBLICATIONS

OF

WILLIAM ANDREWS & CO.,

5 FARRINGDON AVENUE, LONDON.

The Bygone Series.

In this series the following volumes are included, and issued at 7s. 6d. each. Demy 8vo, cloth gilt.

These books have been favourably reviewed in the leading critical journals of England and America.

Carefully written articles by recognised authorities are included on history, castles, abbeys, biography, romantic episodes, legendary lore, traditional stories, curious customs, folk-lore, etc., etc.

The works are illustrated by eminent artists, and by the reproduction of quaint pictures of the olden time.

BYGONE BERKSHIRE, edited by Rev. P. H. Ditchfield, M.A., F.S.A.

BYGONE CHESHIRE, edited by William Andrews.

BYGONE DEVONSHIRE, by the Rev. Hilderic Friend.

BYGONE DURHAM, edited by William Andrews.

BYGONE GLOUCESTERSHIRE, edited by William Andrews.

BYGONE HERTFORDSHIRE, edited by William Andrews.

BYGONE LEICESTERSHIRE, edited by William Andrews.

BYGONE LINCOLNSHIRE (2 vols), edited by William Andrews.

BYGONE MIDDLESEX, edited by William Andrews.

BYGONE NORFOLK, edited by William Andrews.

BYGONE NORTHUMBERLAND, edited by William Andrews.

BYGONE NOTTINGHAMSHIRE, by William Stevenson.

BYGONE SCOTLAND, by David Maxwell, C.E.

BYGONE SOMERSETSHIRE, edited by Cuming Walters.

BYGONE SOUTHWARK, by Mrs. E. Boger.

BYGONE SUFFOLK, edited by Cuming Walters.

BYGONE SURREY, edited by George Clinch and S. W. Kershaw, F.S.A.

BYGONE SUSSEX, by W. E. A. Axon.

BYGONE WARWICKSHIRE, edited by William Andrews.

BYGONE YORKSHIRE, edited by William Andrews.

England in the Days of Old.

By WILLIAM ANDREWS, F.R.H.S.

Demy 8vo., 7s. 6d. Numerous Illustrations.

THIS volume is one of unusual interest and value to the lover of olden days and ways, and can hardly fail to interest and instruct the reader. It recalls many forgotten episodes, scenes, characters, manners, customs, etc., in the social and domestic life of England.

CONTENTS :—When Wigs were Worn—Powdering the Hair—Men Wearing Muffs—Concerning Corporation Customs—Bribes for the Palate —Rebel Heads on City Gates—Burial at Cross Roads—Detaining the Dead for Debt—A Nobleman's Household in Tudor Times—Bread and Baking in Bygone Days—Arise, Mistress, Arise !—The Turnspit—A Gossip about the Goose —Bells as Time-Tellers—The Age of Snuffing—State Lotteries— Bear-Baiting—Morris Dancers—The Folk-Lore of Midsummer Eve— Harvest Home—Curious Charities—An Old-Time Chronicler.

LIST OF ILLUSTRATIONS :—The House of Commons in the time of Sir Robert Walpole—Egyptian Wig—The Earl of Albemarle—Campaign Wig —Periwig with Tail—Ramillie-Wig—Pig-tail Wig—Bag-Wig—Archbishop Tilotson—Heart-Breakers—A Barber's Shop in the time of Queen Elizabeth —With and Without a Wig—Stealing a Wig—Man with Muff, 1693— Burying the Mace at Nottingham—The Lord Mayor of York escorting Princess Margaret—The Mayor of Wycombe going to the Guildhall— Woman wearing a Scold's Bridle—The Brank—Andrew Marvell—Old London Bridge, shewing heads of rebels on the gate—Axe, Block, and Executioner's Mask—Margaret Roper taking leave of her father, Sir Thomas More—Rebel Heads, from a print published in 1746—Temple Bar in Dr. Johnson's time—Micklegate Bar, York—Clock, Hampton Court Palace— Drawing a Lottery in the Guildhall, 1751—Advertising the Last State Lottery—Partaking of the Pungent Pinch—Morris Dance, from a painted window at Betley—Morris Dance, temp. James I.—A Whitsun Morris Dance—Bear Garden, or Hope Theatre, 1647—The Globe Theatre, temp. Elizabeth—Plan of Bankside early in the Seventeenth Century—John Stow's Monument.

A carefully prepared Index enables the reader to refer to the varied and interesting contents of the book.

Bygone Punishments.

By William Andrews.

Demy 8vo, cloth gilt, 7s. 6d.   Numerous Illustrations.

Contents :—Hanging—Hanging in Chains—Hanging, Drawing, and Quartering—Pressing to Death—Drowning—Burning to Death—Boiling to Death—Beheading—The Halifax Gibbet—The Scottish Maiden—Mutilation—Branding—The Pillory—Punishing Authors and Burning Books—Finger Pillory—The Jougs—The Stocks—The Drunkard's Cloak—Whipping and Whipping-Posts—Public Penance—The Repentance Stool—The Ducking Stool—The Brank, or Scold's Bridle—Riding the Stang—Index.

" A book of great interest."—*Manchester Courier.*

" Crowded with extraordinary facts."—*Birmingham Daily Gazette.*

"Contains much that is curious and interesting both to the student of history and social reformer."—*Lancashire Daily Express.*

" Full of curious lore, sought out and arranged with much industry."—*The Scotsman.*

" Mr. Andrews' volume is admirably produced, and contains a collection of curious illustrations, representative of many of the punishments he describes, which contribute towards making it one of the most curious and entertaining books that we have perused for a long time."—*Norfolk Chronicle.*

"Those who wish to obtain a good general idea on the subject of criminal punishment in days long past, will obtain it in this well-printed and stoutly-bound volume."—*Daily Mail.*

" Mr. William Andrews, of Hull, is an indefatigable searcher amongst the byways of ancient English history, and it would be difficult to name an antiquary who, along his chosen lines, has made so thoroughly interesting and instructive the mass of facts a painstaking industry has brought to light.   For twenty-five years he has been delving into the subject of Bygone Punishments, and is now one of the best authorities upon obsolete systems of jurisdiction and torture, for torture was, in various forms, the main characteristic of punishment in the good old times.   The reformation of the person punished was a far more remote object of retribution than it is with us, and even with us reform is very much a matter of sentiment. Punishment was intended to be punishment to the individual in the first place, and in the second a warning to the rest.   It is a gruesome study, but Mr. Andrews nowhere writes for mere effect.   As an antiquary ought to do, he has made the collection of facts and their preservation for modern students of history in a clear, straightforward narrative his main object, and in this volume he keeps to it consistently.   Every page is therefore full of curious, out-of-the-way facts, with authorities and references amply quoted."—*Yorkshire Post.*

Literary Byways.

By WILLIAM ANDREWS.

Demy 8vo., cloth gilt, 7s. 6d.

CONTENTS:—Authors at Work—The Earnings of Authors—"Declined with Thanks"—Epigrams on Authors—Poetical Graces—Poetry on Panes—English Folk Rhymes—The Poetry of Toast Lists and Menu Cards—Toasts and Toasting—Curious American Old-Time Gleanings —The Earliest American Poetess : Anne Bradstreet—A Playful Poet : Miss Catherine Fanshawe—A Popular Song Writer : Mrs. John Hunter—A Poet of the Poor : Mary Pyper—The Poet of the Fisher-Folk : Mrs. Susan K. Phillips—A Poet and Novelist of the People : Thomas Miller—The Cottage Countess—The Compiler of " Old Moore's Almanack " : Henry Andrews—James Nayler, the Mad Quaker, who claimed to be the Messiah—A Biographical Romance : Swan's Strange Story—Short Letters—Index.

"An interesting volume."—*Church Bells.*

"Turn where you will, there is information and entertainment in this book."—*Birmingham Daily Gazette.*

" The volume is most enjoyable."—*Perthshire Advertiser.*

" The volume consists of entertaining chapters written in a chatty style."—*Daily Advertiser.*

" A readable volume about authors and books. . . . Like Mr. Andrews's other works, the book shows wide out-of-the-way reading." —*Glasgow Herald.*

" Dull after-dinner speakers should be compelled to peruse this volume, and ornament their orations and per-orations with its gems." —*Sunday Times.*

" An entertaining volume. . . . No matter where the book is opened, the reader will find some amusing and instructive matter." —*Dundee Advertiser.*

" Readable and entertaining."—*Notes and Queries.*

" Mr. Andrews delights in the production of the pleasant, gossipy order of books. He is well qualified, indeed, to do so, for he is pains-taking in the collection of interesting literary facts, methodical in setting them forth, and he loves books with genuine ardour."— *Aberdeen Free Press.*

" We heartily commend this volume to the attention of readers who are in any way interested in literature."—*Scots Pictorial.*

The Church Treasury of History, Custom, Folk-Lore, etc.

Edited by WILLIAM ANDREWS.

Demy 8vo., 7s. 6d. Numerous Illustrations.

Contents :—Stave-Kirks—Curious Churches of Cornwall—Holy Wells—Hermits and Hermit Cells—Church Wakes—Fortified Church Towers—The Knight Templars: their Churches and their Privileges—English Mediæval Pilgrimages—Pilgrims' Signs—Human Skin on Church Doors—Animals of the Church in Wood, Stone, and Bronze—Queries in Stones—Pictures in Churches—Flowers and the Rites of the Church—Ghost Layers and Ghost Laying—Church Walks—Westminster Waxworks—Index. Numerous Illustrations.

" It is a work that will prove interesting to the clergy and churchmen generally, and to all others who have an antiquarian turn of mind, or like to be regaled occasionally by reading old-world customs and anecdotes."—*Church Family Newspaper.*

" Mr. Andrews has given us some excellent volumes of Church lore, but none quite so good as this. The subjects are well chosen. They are treated brightly and with considerable detail, and they are well illustrated. . . . . . Mr. Andrews is himself responsible for some of the most interesting papers, but all his helpers have caught his own spirit, and the result is a volume full of information well and pleasantly put."—*London Quarterly Review.*

." Those who seek information regarding curious and quaint relics or customs will find much to interest them in this book. The illustrations are good."—*Publishers' Circular.*

" An excellent and entertaining book."—*Newcastle Daily Leader.*

" The book will be welcome to every lover of archæological lore."—*Liverpool Daily Post.*

" The volume is of a most informing and suggestive character, abounding in facts not easy of access to the ordinary reader, and enhanced with illustrations of a high order of merit, and extremely numerous."—*Birmingham Daily Gazette.*

" The contents of the volume are very good."—*Leeds Mercury.*

" The volume is sure to meet with a cordial reception."—*Manchester Courier.*

" A fascinating book."—*Stockport Advertiser.*

" Mr. Andrews has brought together much curious matter."—*Manchester Guardian.*

" The book is a very readable one, and will receive a hearty welcome."—*Herts. Advertiser.*

" Mr. William Andrews has been able to give us a very acceptable and useful addition to the books which deal with the curiosities of Church lore, and for this deserves our hearty thanks. The manner in which the book is printed and illustrated also commands our admiration."—*Norfolk Chronicle.*

Historic Dress of the Clergy.

BY THE REV. GEO. S. TYACK, B.A.,

Author of "The Cross in Ritual, Architecture, and Art."

Crown, cloth extra, 3s. 6d.

The work contains thirty-three illustrations from ancient monuments, rare manuscripts, and other sources.

"A very painstaking and very valuable volume on a subject which is just now attracting much attention. Mr. Tyack has collected a large amount of information from sources not available to the unlearned, and has put together his materials in an attractive way. The book deserves and is sure to meet with a wide circulation."—*Daily Chronicle.*

"This book is written with great care, and with an evident knowledge of history. It is well worth the study of all who wish to be better informed upon a subject which the author states in his preface gives evident signs of a lively and growing interest."—*Manchester Courier.*

"Those who are interested in the Dress of the Clergy will find full information gathered together here, and set forth in a lucid and scholarly way."—*Glasgow Herald.*

"We are glad to welcome yet another volume from the author of 'The Cross in Ritual, Architecture, and Art.' His subject, chosen widely and carried out comprehensively, makes this a valuable book of reference for all classes. It is only the antiquary and the ecclesiologist who can devote time and talents to research of this kind, and Mr. Tyack has done a real and lasting service to the Church of England by collecting so much useful and reliable information upon the dress of the clergy in all ages, and offering it to the public in such a popular form. We do not hesitate to recommend this volume as the most reliable and the most comprehensive illustrated guide to the history and origin of the canonical vestments and other dress worn by the clergy, whether ecclesiastical, academical, or general, while the excellent work in typography and binding make it a beautiful gift-book."—*Church Bells.*

"A very lucid history of ecclesiastical vestments from Levitical times to the present day."—*Pall Mall Gazette.*

"The book can be recommended to the undoubtedly large class of persons who are seeking information on this and kindred subjects."—*The Times.*

"The work may be read either as pastime or for instruction, and is worthy of a place in the permanent section of any library. The numerous illustrations, extensive contents table and index, and beautiful workmanship, both in typography and binding, are all features of attraction and utility."
Dundee Advertiser.

The Miracle Play in England,

An Account of the Early Religious Drama.

By SIDNEY W. CLARKE, Barrister-at-Law.

Crown 8vo., 3s. 6d. Illustrated.

In bygone times the Miracle Play formed an important feature in the religious life of England. To those taking an interest in the history of the Church of England, this volume will prove useful. The author has given long and careful study to this subject, and produced a reliable and readable book, which can hardly fail to interest and instruct the reader. It is a volume for general reading, and for a permanent place in the reference library.

Contents :—The Origin of Drama—The Beginnings of English Drama —The York Plays—The Wakefield Plays—The Chester Plays—The Coventry Plays—Other English Miracle Plays—The Production of a Miracle Play—The Scenery, Properties, and Dresses— Appendix—The Order of the York Plays—Extract from City Register of York, 1426— The Order of the Wakefield Plays—The Order of the Chester Plays— The Order of the Grey Friars' Plays at Coventry—A Miracle Play in a Puppet Show —Index.

"Mr. Clarke has chosen a most interesting subject, one that is attractive alike to the student, the historian, and the general reader . . . . A most interesting volume, and a number of quaint illustrations add to its value."--*Birmingham Daily Gazette.*

"The book should be useful to many."—*Manchester Guardian.*

"An admirable work."—*Eastern Morning News.*

"Mr. Sidney Clarke's concise monograph in 'The Miracle Play in England' is another of the long and interesting series of antiquarian volumes for popular reading issued by the same publishing house. The author briefly sketches the rise and growth of the 'Miracle' or 'Mystery' play in Europe and in England ; and gives an account of the series or cycle of these curious religious dramas—the forerunners of the modern secular play—performed at York, Wakefield, Chester, Coventry, and other towns in the middle ages. But his chief efforts are devoted to giving a sketch of the manner of production, and the scenery, properties, and dresses of the old miracle play, as drawn from the minute account books of the craft and trade guilds and other authentic records of the period. Mr. Clarke has gone to the best sources for his information, and the volume, illustrated by quaint cuts, is an excellent compendium of information on a curious byeway of literature and art."—*The Scotsman.*

A Book About Bells.

By the Rev. GEO. S. TYACK, b.a.,

Author of the "Historic Dress of the Clergy," etc.

Crown, cloth extra, 6s.

Contents :—Invention of Bells—Bell Founding and Bell Founders—Dates and Names of Bells—The Decoration of Bells—Some Noteworthy Bells—The Loss of Old Bells—Towers and Campaniles—Bell-Ringing and Bell-Ringers—The Church-Going Bell—Bells at Christian Festivals and Fasts—The Epochs of Man's Life Marked by the Bells—The Blessings and the Cursings of the Bells—Bells as Time-Markers—Secular Uses of Church and other Bells—Small Bells, Secular and Sacred—Carillons—Belfry Rhymes and Legends—Index of Subjects, Index of Places.

THIRTEEN FULL-PAGE PLATES.

" A most useful and interesting book. . . . All who are interested in bells will, we feel confident, read it with pleasure and profit."—*Church Family Newspaper.*

"A pleasing, graceful, and scholarly book. . . . . A handsome volume which will be prized by the antiquary, and can be perused with delight and advantage by the general reader."—*Notes and Queries.*

" ' A Book About Bells' can be heartily commended."—*Pall Mall Gazette.*

"An excellent and entertaining book, which we commend to the attention not only of those who are specially interested in the subject of bells, but to all lovers of quaint archæological lore."—*Glasgow Herald.*

" The book is well printed and artistic in form."—*Manchester Courier.*

" ' A Book About Bells' is destined to be the work of reference on the subject, and it ought to find a home on the shelves of every library."—*Northern Gazette.*

" The task Mr. Tyack has set himself, he has carried out admirably, and throughout care and patient research are apparent."—*Lynn News.*

" We heartily recommend our readers to procure this volume."—*The Churchwoman.*

" An entertaining work."—*Yorkshire Post.*

" ' A Book About Bells' will interest almost everyone. Antiquaries will find in it an immense store of information : but the general reader will equally feel that it is a book well worth reading from beginning to end."—*The News,* Edited by the Rev. Charles Bullock, b.d.

" An excellent work."—*Stockton Herald.*

" It is a well-written work, and it is sure to be popular."—*Hull Christian Voice.*

" Covers the whole field of bell-lore."—*Scotsman.*

" Most interesting and finely illustrated."—*Birmingham Daily Gazette.*

Legal Lore: Curiosities of Law and Lawyers.

EDITED BY WILLIAM ANDREWS, F.R.H.S.

Demy 8vo., Cloth extra, 7s. 6d.

CONTENTS :—Bible Law—Sanctuaries—Trials in Superstitious Ages—On Symbols—Law Under the Feudal System—The Manor and Manor Law—Ancient Tenures—Laws of the Forest—Trial by Jury in Old Times—Barbarous Punishments—Trials of Animals—Devices of the Sixteenth Century Debtors—Laws Relating to the Gipsies—Commonwealth Law and Lawyers—Cock-Fighting in Scotland—Cockieleerie Law—Fatal Links—Post-Mortem Trials—Island Laws—The Little Inns of Court—Obiter.

"There are some very amusing and curious facts concerning law and lawyers. We have read with much interest the articles on Sanctuaries, Trials in Superstitious Ages, Ancient Tenures, Trials by Jury in Old Times, Barbarous Punishments, and Trials of Animals, and can heartily recommend the volume to those who wish for a few hours' profitable diversion in the study of what may be called the light literature of the law."—*Daily Mail.*

"Most amusing and instructive reading."—*The Scotsman.*

"The contents of the volume are extremely entertaining, and convey not a little information on ancient ideas and habits of life. While members of the legal profession will turn to the work for incidents with which to illustrate an argument or point a joke, laymen will enjoy its vivid descriptions of old-fashioned proceedings and often semi-barbaric ideas to obligation and rectitude."—*Dundee Advertiser.*

"The subjects chosen are extremely interesting, and contain a quantity of out-of-the-way and not easily accessible information. . . . Very tastefully printed and bound."—*Birmingham Daily Gazette.*

"The book is handsomely got up; the style throughout is popular and clear, and the variety of its contents, and the individuality of the writers gave an added charm to the work."—*Daily Free Press.*

"The book is interesting both to the general reader and the student."—*Cheshire Notes and Queries.*

"Those who care only to be amused will find plenty of entertainment in this volume, while those who regard it as a work of reference will rejoice at the variety of material, and appreciate the careful indexing."—*Dundee Courier.*

"Very interesting subjects, lucidly and charmingly written. The versatility of the work assures for it a wide popularity."—*Northern Gazette.*

"A happy and useful addition to current literature."—*Norfolk Chronicle.*

"The book is a very fascinating one, and it is specially interesting to students of history as showing the vast changes which, by gradual course of development have been brought about both in the principles and practice of the law."—*The Evening Gazette.*

Antiquities and Curiosities of the Church.

Edited by WILLIAM ANDREWS, f.r.h.s.

Demy 8vo., 7s. 6d. Numerous Illustrations.

Contents :—Church History and Historians—Supernatural Interference in Church Building—Ecclesiastical Symbolism in Architecture—Acoustic Jars—Crypts—Heathen Customs at Christian Feasts—Fish and Fasting—Shrove-tide and Lenten Customs—Wearing Hats in Church—The Stool of Repentance—Cursing by Bell, Book, and Candle—Pulpits—Church Windows—Alms-Boxes and Alms-Dishes—Old Collecting Boxes—Gargoyles—Curious Vanes—People and Steeple Rhymes—Sun-Dials—Jack of the Clock-House—Games in Churchyards—Circular Churchyards—Church and Churchyard Charms and Cures—Yew Trees in Churchyards.

" A very entertaining work."—*Leeds Mercury.*

" A well-printed, handsome, and profusely illustrated work."—*Norfolk Chronicle.*

" There is much curious and interesting reading in this popular volume, which moreover has a useful index."—*Glasgow Herald.*

" The contents of the volume is exceptionally good reading, and crowded with out-of-the way, useful, and well selected information on a subject which has an undying interest."—*Birmingham Mercury.*

" In concluding this notice it is only the merest justice to add that every page of it abounds with rare and often amusing information, drawn from the most accredited sources. It also abounds with illustrations of our old English authors, and it is likely to prove welcome not only to the Churchman, but to the student of folk-lore and of poetical literature."—*Morning Post.*

" We can recommend this volume to all who are interested in the notable and curious things that relate to churches and public worship in this and other countries."—*Newcastle Daily Journal.*

" It is very handsomely got up and admirably printed, the letterpress being beautifully clear."—*Lincoln Mercury.*

" The book is well indexed."—*Daily Chronicle.*

" By delegating certain topics to those most capable of treating them, the editor has the satisfaction of presenting the best available information in a very attractive manner."—*Dundee Aavertiser.*

" It must not be supposed that the book is of interest only to Churchmen, although primarily so, for it treats in such a skilful and instructive manner with ancient manners and customs as to make it an invaluable book of reference to all who are concerned in the seductive study of antiquarian subjects."—*Chester Courant.*

`Curious Church Customs,

AND COGNATE SUBJECTS.

Edited by WILLIAM ANDREWS, F.R.H.S.

Demy 8vo, price 7s. 6d.

CONTENTS :—Sports in Churches—Holy Day Customs—Church Bells : When and Why They were Rung—Inscriptions on Bells—Laws of the Belfry—Ringers' Jugs—Customs and Superstitions of Baptism—Marriage Customs—Burial Customs—Concerning the Churchyard—Altars in Churches —The Rood Loft and its Uses—Armour in Churches—Beating the Bounds —The Story of the Croiser—Bishops in Battle—The Cloister and its Story —Shorthand in Church—Reminiscences of our Village Church—Index.

"The book is an interesting addition to antiquarian and popular literature."—*The Scotsman.*

"A highly interesting work. . . . There are in all nineteen chapters, containing a large and varied amount of information on many subjects, respecting which the general public are not too well informed."—*Somerset County Herald.*

"An extremely interesting work."—*The Bazaar.*

"A distinctly valuable addition to the literature dealing with the antiquities of the Church."—*The Evening Post.*

"A varied and comprehensive volume, evidently the outcome of much patient research."—*The World.*

"The value of the book is greatly enhanced by an admirable index."— *North Eastern Gazette.*

"It is as interesting as a novel."—*Blackburn Standard.*

"We are indebted to Mr. Andrews for an invaluable addition to our library of folk-lore, and we do not think that many who take it up will skip a single page."—*Dundee Advertiser.*

"A thoroughly excellent volume."—*Publishers' Circular.*

"Very interesting."—*To-Day.*

"Mr. Andrews is too practised an historian not to have made the most of his subject."—*Review of Reviews.*

"A handsomely got up and interesting volume."—*The Fireside.*

The Prime Minister of Würtemburg.

By ELLER,

Author of " Ingatherings."

Crown 8vo. Bound in cloth extra, 3s. 6d.

" This anonymously-written story is of much power, and presents to us a picture of the Government in Würtemburg a hundred and sixty years ago, when the reigning Duke Alexandra, in his indulgence and foolishly fond treatment of his Cabinet Minister and Finance Director, the Jew Siece, has placed his subjects at the mercy of a crafty and designing man. How his object to overthrow the hero of the story, Gustave Lanbek, and his father, by forcing him to take an office which would bring him the contempt of his friends and the hatred of the people, was ultimately frustrated by the encompassing of his own ruin, is a plot which is developed and completed in a most dramatic manner. There is, too, a thread of love-making, the course of which runs by no means smoothly, deftly introduced into the main theme of the story, which lightens and relieves the plot. The book is one which we have thoroughly enjoyed, and both author and publishers are to be complimented upon the production of a volume effectively written and attractively printed and bound."—*Norfolk Chronicle.*

" The book has the great merit of soon interesting the reader. The get-up of the book reflects credit upon the publishers."—*Daily Mail.*

" A pretty story well told."—*Hull News.*

" Ingatherings."

By ELLER.

Crown 8vo. Elegantly bound in cloth extra, 3s 6d.

" This is an exceedingly interesting collection of writings in prose and poetry. The book opens with a quaint story descriptive of the manner in which a young German nobleman, by his purity and goodness, delivered an old baron and his lovely daughter from the power of the evil one. Among the other pieces of prose are 'The Voices of Nature,' 'A Dream,' 'A Reverie,' each of which proves the author to possess considerable ability. Their artistic style is delightfully refreshing. The poems are for the most part original, but there are one or two gems from the pens of Goethe, Schiller, and other master-minds. The publishers are to be congratulated on the general get-up of the book."--*Chester Courant.*

The Church Bells of Holderness.

By GODFREY RICHARD PARK.

Crown 8vo, cloth extra.   Only 800 copies printed.

CONTENTS :—History—Legends—Marriage Bell—Passing Bell—Priest's Bell—Litany Bell—Sermon Bell—Saunce Bell—Sanctus Bell—Sacring Bell—Jesus Bell—Howslinge Bell—The Arc Bell—Curfew Bell—Harvest Bell—Pancake Bell—Christmas Day—Good Friday—Easter Sunday—All Hallows'—Royal Oak Day—Gowrie Plot—Gunpowder Plot—Change Ringing—Dedication of Churches—Inscriptions on the Church Bells of Holderness—Dedication of Church Bells—Index.

" To all who are interested in church bells Mr. Park's book will afford interesting reading."—*Hull Times.*

" A capital volume includes much out-of-the-way information on the bell in history, legend, and custom, and cannot fail to entertain all who take an interest in the church bells." —*Leamington Advertiser.*

" Mr. Park's volume makes a welcome contribution to antiquarian literature."—*Hull Christian Voice.*

Essex in the Days of Old.

EDITED BY JOHN T. PAGE.

Demy 8vo, cloth gilt, 7s. 6d.   Numerous illustrations.

CONTENTS :—Witchcraft in Essex—Charles Dickens and Chigwell—Hadleigh Castle—Daniel Defoe in Essex—Harbottle Grimston, Puritan and Patriot—In the Reign of Terror—John Locke and Oates—The Homes and Haunts of Elizabeth Fry—The Notorious Dean of Bocking and the " Eikon Basilike "—Barking Abbey—The Round Church of Little Maplestead—Waltham Holy Cross—Queen Elizabeth in Essex—The Salmons and Haddocks of Leigh—The Dutch Refugees and the Bay and Say Trade —John Strype and Leyton—The Brass of Archbishop Harsnett—Old Southend—The Bartlow Hills—Index.

" An extremely interesting and useful contribution to historic literature." --*East Anglian Times.*   ·

" An attractive volume."—*Norfolk Chronicle.*

" The volume is choicely illustrated, and should attract readers far beyond the county of which it treats."—*Birmingham Daily Gazette.*

" It is a readable and useful book."—*The Times.*

The Doomed Ship; or, The Wreck in the Arctic Regions.

By WILLIAM HURTON.

Crown 8vo., Elegantly Bound, Gilt extra, 3s. 6d.

"There is no lack of adventures, and the writer has a matter-of-fact way of telling them."—*Spectator.*

" 'The Doomed Ship,' by William Hurton, is a spirited tale of adventures in the old style of sea-stories. Mr. Hurton seems to enter fully into the manliness of sea life."—*Idler.*

"It is not surprising to learn that the Arctic boom has created a great demand for books of this class, and that the volume before us in particular is selling rapidly. It is entitled 'The Doomed Ship, or the Wreck in the Arctic Regions.' By William Hurton. (London : William Andrew. and Co., 5, Farringdon Avenue, E.C. Three Shillings and Sixpence). It is of general interest, but it is written in an attractive style, nicely printed, and handsomely bound. Brimful of adventures in the ice-bound regions of the North, it also gives a great deal of information which the reading public are taking a great interest in since Dr. Nansen's exploits have been brought before the world. The story is told in the form of a narrative by the nephew of the captain of the 'good barque Lady Emily, chartered from Hull to Tromso, in Holland.' The vessel sailed on a Friday—an unlucky day in the eyes of superstitious sailors, and which to their minds accounted for the dire experiences which afterwards befell the vessel and the crew. The vessel was laden with coals and salt, and, after leaving Tromso, was to proceed to St. Petersburg to ship timber and deals for the return voyage. She had twenty-two hands, and at Tromso took on board a passenger for Copenhagen, in the person of a young Danish lady, Oriana Neilsen by name. Chepini, an Italian lad, in revenge for being flogged by the captain's orders, so manipulated the compass that the ship was taken hopelessly out of her course. Chepini is hung up to the yard arm. The vessel is at the time surrounded by icebergs, a gale springs up, and she is forced on to one of the bergs and remains fast by the bow, while a mutiny occurs among the crew, which is not quelled till the mutineers are killed, as well as the captain and cook. Oriana plays a noble part in the affair, and the nephew of the captain and she take command of the remainder of the crew, now consisting only of "Blackbird Jim" and an Irishman and a Scotchman. As the ship's bows were stove in, and it was evident that whenever she cleared the iceberg she would go down, the longboat was cleared away, and all the provisions and other necessaries put into it. The survivors landed on an ice-bound shore, and the story of their adventures, discoveries, and subsequent rescue does not contain a dull page. Oriana is the heroine throughout, and the late captain's nephew of course falls in love with her. When they return to civilisation the couple are, of course, married, and they, also of course, live happily ever afterwards. All the same, the development of this state of affairs comes naturally enough in the narrative, which is, as we have already indicated, full of interest."—*Eastern Morning News.*

"The interesting story ends in a satisfactory manner." -*Dundee Advertiser.*

www.ingramcontent.com/pod-product-compliance
Lightning Source LLC
Chambersburg PA
CBHW020501270326
41926CB00008B/694